Workbook/Lab Manual

to accompany

Deutsch heute

Grundstufe / Fourth Edition

Jack Moeller
Oakland University

Helmut Liedloff
Southern Illinois University

Barbara Beckman Sharon

Proficiency Cards by Cynthia Hall Westhof

Houghton Mifflin Company   Boston

Dallas   Geneva, Illinois   Palo Alto   Princeton, New Jersey

Credits

The authors and editors of the *Deutsch heute, Fourth Edition* Workbook/Lab Manual would like to thank the following companies and organizations for granting permission to reproduce copyrighted material:

p. 36: Kare Regale, München.

p. 37: Zeleste Tanzbar, Berlin.

p. 41: Aktion Zeitschriftenanzeige, Bonn 2/Bad Godesberg.

p. 42: Metropol—Tango Bar, Berlin; Dr.med. Hans-Joachim Siebert, Bewegungsbad Schnelsen, Hamburg; Günther Poehling, Hamburger Tennisschule, Hamburg.

p. 48: Magi Wechsler, Zürich.

p. 64: Lexika Verlag, München.

p. 74: Wise Publications/Music Sales Corporation, New York, N.Y.

p. 76: Bayrischer Heilbäderverband, Bad Kissingen; Kurdirektion Mittenwald, Mittenwald.

p. 82: Landratsamt Tuttlingen—Umweltamt, Tuttlingen.

p. 90: "99" nein ti nein, Hamburg; Privatbrauerei Kesselring, Marktsteft am Main.

p. 98: Optik am Kleistpark, Berlin.

p. 103: Official Tourist Office of Berne, Switzerland.

p. 106: Lufthansa German Airlines.

p. 108: Universitätsbuchhandlung Dr. Joseph C. Witsch Nachf., Köln.

p. 109: Cycles Peugeot, Postfach 1220, 5063 Overath 1, West-Germany.

p. 112: Rechsteiner Personalberatung, Zürich.

p. 114: aus: Kalender *Dumme Sprüche für Gescheite*, mit freundlicher Genehmigung des Friedrich W. Heye Verlags, Hamburg–München.

p. 118: Heinen-Verlag, Stolkgasse 24–45, 5000 Köln 1, West-Germany.

p. 119: Dütt & Datt Hobby- und Jugendbasar, Lübeck.

p. 120: from: *Urlaub—Tips für Ihre Ferienreise.*

p. 124: Deutsche Bundesbahn, Mainz.

p. 138: Kino Wellenberg, Zürich.

p. 140: Il Pescatore Café & Ristorante, Berlin; Indisches Restaurant Golden Temple & Ajanta—Indian Food Store, Berlin; Koisago Curry-House, Berlin.

Drawings by George Ulrich and Anne Burgess.

Cover photo by J.H. Neumann/Bildarchiv Bucher, Munich, West Germany

Printed in the U.S.A.

Library of Congress Catalog Card Number: 87-80878

ISBN: 0-395-44871-9

DEFGHIJ-A-9543210/89

Contents

Introduction

The Workbook/Lab Manual to accompany **Deutsch heute: Grundstufe, Fourth Edition,** is designed to help students improve their reading and writing skills, reinforce their listening comprehension skills, and enhance their cognition of the grammatical features of German. The Workbook/Lab Manual is divided into four main sections: (1) a Lab Manual, (2) a Workbook, (3) Self Tests with an Answer Key, and (4) a set of 60 Proficiency Cards. Each section is divided into an **Einführung** and fourteen **Kapitel** that correspond to the chapters of the text. The exercises and activities in these four sections reinforce and review vocabulary, culture, and structures presented in the corresponding and previous chapters of the text, by recombining material from the **Bausteine, Sie haben das Wort, Lesestücke,** and **Grammatik und Übungen.**

Workbook/Lab Manual exercises can be assigned in several ways: Some activities can be done profitably while students are working with the corresponding material in a specific chapter, while other activities can serve well as review. The Self-Tests are ideal for end-of-chapter review.

Pages in the Workbook/Lab Manual are perforated so that students may hand in their work for correction by the instructor. The instructor may also provide students with the answers by duplicating and distributing relevant pages from the Answer Key (a separate component). Alternate answers are provided where appropriate.

Lab Manual (pages 1–30)

The Lab Manual contains material that is coordinated with the **Übungen zum Hörverständnis** in the tape program. The script for these listening comprehension exercises is printed in the Tapescript/Answer Key. The exercises consist of new aural material based on the dialogues and readings in each chapter. Exercises include true-false statements about the **Lesestück** and about conversations and stories heard on the tape, logical/illogical response, and dictations. In general, students respond to recorded material by checking correct answers or writing short answers in the Lab Manual.

Workbook (pages 33–142)

The Workbook provides students with guided practice in improving their writing skills in German. Exercises include dialogue or sentence completion, rewriting sentences, answering questions, building sentences or paragaphs from guidelines, and creating short compositions. Some exercises, including **Sie haben das Wort,** encourage students to express their own moods, opinions, and ideas and to speculate on what they would do in a particular situation. Other exercises are based on line art and realia, including maps, tables, and charts; some activities offer extra reading practice and new cultural information. Vocabulary sophistication is developed by exercises that require students to supply synonyms, antonyms or definitions, or to form new words with suffixes and prefixes.

Self-Tests (pages 143–165)

The Self-Tests help students determine whether they are ready for the chapter test by giving them an opportunity to review structures and vocabulary. Doing the Self-Tests, either individually or in class, will enable students to see whether they have understood the grammatical features introduced in the chapter and whether they can apply their understanding of the grammatical principles. Students will need to use a separate answer sheet for the Self-Tests. An answer key appears at the back of the Workbook/Lab Manual for self-correction.

Proficiency Cards (pages 167–200)

New to the Fourth Edition of **Deutsch heute,** this set of 60 activity cards has been designed to help students develop oral proficiency in German. By providing a meaningful context and task for each interaction, the cards can be used to stimulate active, spontaneous communication involving oral skills learned in the text.

There are four cards for every chapter of **Deutsch heute,** including the **Einführung.** Within each chapter, the tasks described on the cards are sequenced to move from controlled situations to free conversations. The first card for every chapter is a short warm-up activity, the second and third cards involve role-playing, directed dialogues, and pair work activities, and the fourth card, the **Kaffeestunde,** is intended for general conversation.

Warm-ups. These cards involve brief, controlled discussions using ideas, vocabulary, and structures that tie in with the activities presented in the second and third cards. The ideal number of people required for the activity is specified on the cards; this can be modified according to class size. The warm-ups should be kept to about five minutes.

Directed activity cards. The second and third cards present situations that require a specific number of people to interact with each other. These situations integrate the vocabulary, grammar, and themes of the chapter. The direction line indicates who is involved, e.g., *You are trying to convince a friend of yours to go with you to Austria.* As there are two people indicated in the direction line, this card should be worked on in pairs. The students read the card together and decide who will take which role. They then develop a conversation according to the situation presented. Many of the cards present general situations in which the context is given but students develop the conversation as they wish. Other cards direct the dialogue according to specific numbered cues (e.g., card 25). Students should read through these together, understand the concepts and meanings that will be expressed, and develop the dialogue without any written notes. They can practice the exchanges a few times together, switching roles until the conversation becomes more fluent.

Kaffeestunde. These activities are the most open-ended. Students are given a topic to talk about with another student. These topics are based on the themes of the chapter. Two suggestions for using these cards are:

1. Use the card for communication work when the chapter is finished or at any other time to review material which was learned in the chapter as a sort of "spot" review.
2. Collect all the **Kaffeestunde** cards and make a booklet. Once a week students can talk with

each other about topics which they are currently learning and can review previous topics. This is the most open-ended review activity for proficiency.

One way to work with the booklets is to hand each student a **Kaffeestunde** booklet. (These should be kept for future **Kaffeestunde** activities.) Students walk around the classroom and, when the instructor indicates, stop and turn to the specified card, and start a conversation about one of the topics on that card. As the class progresses through the book, the **Kaffeestunde** cards can be used to review earlier themes. The conversations about the topics will change each time these cards are used because students' communicative abilities will have developed and students will interact with different partners each time. Rather than being repetitious, the review will resemble a spiral, increasing in complexity each time.

During the **Kaffeestunde,** conversation with a particular partner should be brief (3–4 minutes is probably long enough). The instructor indicates when students should start moving again and when they should stop and strike up a new conversation about a different topic.

To support a feeling of common interest in the oral activities, it is useful to have a group occasionally report to the class what the results of the discussion were, or to have a group recreate the interaction for the class.

The instructor can use the Proficiency Cards to check on a student's progress. In any of the activities above, the instructor can take the role of one of the partners. If this is done each time the cards are used, the instructor will be able to work with every student once in the course of several weeks.

The cards may also be used for more formal oral testing. The instructor may have two or more students complete the tasks on a card, or again the instructor may take on one of the roles. In this way, she/he can direct the interchange more and offer the student being tested particular challenges.

Lab Manual

Einführung

In the directions you will hear the following new words:

Übung	*exercise*
Beispiel	*example*
Fangen wir an!	*Let's begin.*

A. Frage und Antwort°. You will hear six questions, each followed
by two responses. If both responses are the same, place a check mark
in the column marked *same*. If the responses are different, place a check
mark in the column marked *different*.

| question and
answer

Same	**Different**		**Same**	**Different**
➤ _____	✓			
1. ✓	_____	4. ✓	_____
2. _____	✓	5. ✓	_____
3. _____	✓	6. _____	✓

B. Welche Nummer? You will hear ten statements about the items pictured below. Put the
number of each statement under the picture to which it refers.

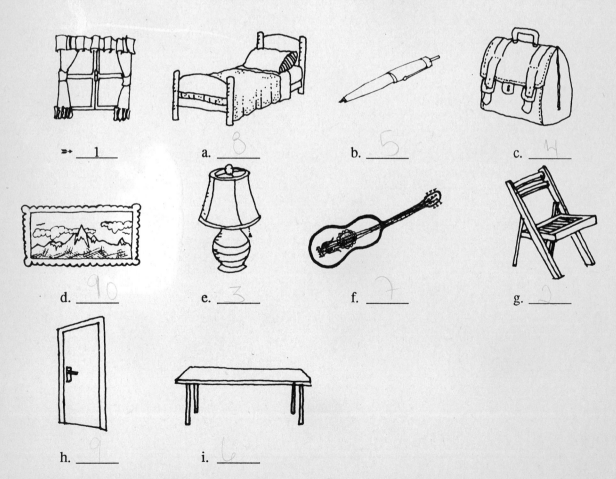

➤ __1__   a. __8__   b. __5__   c. __4__

d. __10__   e. __3__   f. __7__   g. __2__

h. __9__   i. __6__

C. Farben. You will hear nine statements about colors. If a statement is correct, place a check mark in the column marked **Richtig.** If the statement is false, place a check mark in the column marked **Falsch.**

Richtig (true)	Falsch (false)		Richtig	Falsch	
➡ ✓	_____	(die See)			
1. ✓	_____	(die Maus)	5. _____	✓	(die Banane)
2. _____	✓	(die Kohle)	6. ✓	_____	(das Gras)
3. ✓	_____	(die Schokolade)	7. _____	✓	(die Tomate)
4. _____	✓	(das Gras)	8. ✓	✓	(das Papier)

D. Frage und Antwort. You will hear five questions, each followed by two responses. Place a check mark by the letter of the answer that makes sense. You will hear each set of questions and answers twice.

➡ a. _____   b. __✓__

1. a. _____   b. ✓
2. a. _____   b. ✓
3. a. ✓   b. _____
4. a. ✓   b. ✓
5. a. _____   b. ✓

E. Diktat°. Write the words you hear spelled. | *dictation*

➡ *Lampe*

1. adressa   2. danke   3. heißen

Write out the numbers you hear.

1. vier   4   4. neun und funfzig 59
2. elf   11   5. hundert zwölf 112
3. drei und zwanzig 23

Kapitel 1

In the directions you will hear the following new words:

Übung	*exercise*
Beispiel	*example*
Fangen wir an!	*Let's begin.*

A. Ist das logisch? You will hear seven pairs of questions and responses. Place a check mark in the column marked **Logisch** if the response is logical. Place a check mark in the column marked **Unlogisch** if the response to the question is not logical.

Logisch	Unlogisch	Logisch	Unlogisch	Logisch	Unlogisch
➨ ✔	_____				
1. _____	✔	4. _____	✔	6. ✔	_____
2. ✔	_____	5. ✔	_____	7. _____	✔
3. _____	✔				

B. Das Gegenteil°. You will hear seven questions containing an adjective or an adverb. Complete the answer printed in your lab manual by checking the antonym of the adjective or adverb you hear.

the opposite

➨ Nein, er ist ...	✔ a. faul	_____ b. doof
1. Nein, es geht mir ...	✔ a. schlecht	_____ b. ruhig
2. Nein, sie ist ...	_____ a. nervös	✔ b. dumm
3. Nein, er ist ...	_____ a. krank	✔ b. konservativ
4. Nein, sie ist ...	✔ a. lustig	_____ b. müde
5. Nein, es ist ...	_____ a. gut	✔ b. neu
6. Nein, er ist ...	✔ a. ruhig	_____ b. krank
7. Nein, es ist ...	✔ a. klein	_____ b. nett

C. Jürgen. You will hear a brief description of Jürgen and learn what he likes to do. Afterwards, you will hear eight statements. Place a check mark in the column marked **Richtig** if the statement is correct. Place a check mark in the column marked **Falsch** if the statement is incorrect. You will hear the description twice.

	Richtig	Falsch
➨ Jürgen ist 22 Jahre alt.	_____	✔
1. Er ist faul.	✔	_____
2. Er spielt gern Schach.	✔	_____
3. Er treibt nicht gern Sport.	✔	✔
4. Er spielt Fußball.	✔	_____
5. Er spielt Tischtennis.	✔	✔
6. Er geht oft tanzen.	✔	_____
7. Er geht heute abend ins Kino.	_____	✔
8. Er ist müde heute.	✔	_____

D. Diktat. What are Susi and Oliver doing? Oliver runs into Susi on the street, and they talk about various things. Complete their conversation by supplying the missing words, which you will hear on the tape. You will hear the entire dialogue twice.

➡ Tag, Susi, wie _geht's_ ?

– Tag, Oliver, danke, ___sehr gut___ _____ .

– Du, was ___machst___ du heute ___nachmittag___ ?

– Ich ___arbeite___ .

– Hm... Und ___heute abend___ _____ ?

– Nichts ___besonderes___ .

– Spielst du gern ___tischtennis___ ?

– Ja, ___ganz___ gern.

– ___Spielst___ du mit mir?

– Ja, gern.

Kapitel 2

A. Richtig oder falsch? In your lab manual you will see five questions based on the **Lesestück** "Kühl und klein? –Ja und nein." You will hear the questions and three possible answers to each question. Each answer is said twice. Check the letter of each correct answer. A question may have more than one correct answer.

	a	b	c
➤ Wo liegt die Bundesrepublik Deutschland?	✓	✓	___
1. Wo liegt Bonn?	___	___	___
2. Wie ist das Wetter in Deutschland?	___	___	___
3. Wie groß sind die Bundesrepublik und die DDR?	___	___	___
4. Wieviel Einwohner haben die zwei deutschen Staaten?	___	___	___
5. Wer sind die Nachbarn der Bundesrepublik?	___	___	___

B. Das Wetter. You will hear six short conversational exchanges about the weather. In your lab manual you will see a statement based on each exchange. Check **Richtig** if the statement is correct; check **Falsch** if it is incorrect.

	Richtig	Falsch
➤ Es regnet heute.	___	✓
1. Heute ist es kalt.	___	___
2. Heute ist es schön.	___	___
3. Es ist heute kalt.	___	___
4. Morgen ist es bestimmt warm.	___	___
5. Es schneit.	___	___
6. Hoffentlich regnet es morgen wieder.	___	___

C. Welches Wort? You will hear seven words. Check the word in each printed pair that you hear pronounced.

➤ ___✓___ bleiben _____ treiben

1. _____ nett _____ Bett
2. _____ mehr _____ sehr
3. _____ Stadt _____ Staat
4. _____ morgen _____ Norden

5. _____ wieder _____ weiter
6. _____ heiß _____ weiß
7. _____ scheinen _____ schneien

D. Entgegnungen°. You will hear four statements about the weather. *responses*
In your lab manual you will see two possible replies for each statement.
Check the letter of the reply that makes sense.

➤ __✓__ a. Ja, vielleicht regnet es morgen.

_____ b. Ja, morgen regnet es bestimmt auch.

1. _____ a. Ja, leider, und gestern war es noch so schön.

_____ b. Aber morgen regnet es vielleicht.

2. _____ a. Ja, der Wind ist so kalt.

_____ b. Hoffentlich bleibt es so schön.

3. _____ a. Ja, es bleibt bestimmt so heiß.

_____ b. Ja, bestimmt, der Wind ist so kalt heute.

4. _____ a. Jetzt bleibt es bestimmt warm.

_____ b. Aber heute ist es leider wieder so heiß.

E. Ein Telefongespräch°. Dieter calls Ingrid on the telephone. *telephone conver-
sation*
Listen to their conversation, then check the correct answers to the
questions printed in your lab manual. You will hear the conversation
twice.

1. Was macht Ingrid?

_____ a. Sie spielt Schach.

_____ b. Sie ist im Bett und hört Musik.

2. Wie war das Wetter gestern?

_____ a. Naß und kalt.

_____ b. Schön warm.

3. Warum spielt sie nicht mit Dieter Tennis?

_____ a. Sie spielt nicht gern Tennis.

_____ b. Sie ist krank.

4. Wie ist das Wetter heute?

_____ a. Es ist schönes Wetter.

_____ b. Es regnet.

5. Was macht Dieter?

_____ a. Er geht ins Kino.

_____ b. Er spielt vielleicht mit Ute.

Kapitel 3

A. Richtig oder Falsch? You will hear eight statements based on the **Lesestück** "Einkaufen in Deutschland." Check **Richtig** if the statement is correct according to the information in the reading passage. Check **Falsch** if the statement is incorrect.

	Richtig	Falsch		Richtig	Falsch		Richtig	Falsch
1.	_____	_____	4.	_____	_____	7.	_____	_____
2.	_____	_____	5.	_____	_____	8.	_____	_____
3.	_____	_____	6.	_____	_____			

B. Der richtige Laden°. You will hear four short dialogues. For each one, in your lab manual you will see the names of two possible shops or stores where the dialogue might take place. Place a check mark beside the correct location.

| *the right store*

1. _____ Bäckerei   _____ Buchhandlung
2. _____ Supermarkt   _____ Tante-Emma-Laden
3. _____ Metzger   _____ Markt
4. _____ Apotheke   _____ Drogerie

C. Entgegnungen°. You will hear six questions or statements. In your lab manual you will see two possible responses to each. Place a check mark beside the response that makes sense.

| *responses*

1. _____ a. Ja, ich gehe in den Supermarkt.
   _____ b. Ja, ich gehe ins Kino.
2. _____ a. Nein, wir haben noch viel Brot.
   _____ b. Ja, wir brauchen Wurst.
3. _____ a. Gut, ich gehe in den Supermarkt.
   _____ b. Das Brot ist besser bei Müller.
4. _____ a. Ja, geh doch in die Apotheke!
   _____ b. Ja, ich glaube.
5. _____ a. Wieviel brauchst du?
   _____ b. O.K., ich gehe in die Buchhandlung.
6. _____ a. Gut, ich kaufe drei Pfund.
   _____ b. Sonst noch etwas?

D. Diktat: Gabis Geburtstag. Complete the following story about Gabi's birthday by supplying the missing words, which you will hear on the tape. You will hear the entire story twice.

Gabi hat heute _____. Drei _____ kommen zum

Kaffee. Angelika geht in _____. _____ und kauft

für Gabi ein _____ über Frankreich. Das ist leider nicht ganz

_____. Karin hat nicht so viel Geld. Sie geht auf

_____ _____ und kauft schöne

_____. Sie sind ganz _____. Und Susanne kauft

beim _____ viel _____. Jetzt hat auch sie

_____ _____ _____. Aber

bei Gabi ist es sehr _____. Sie _____ Kuchen,

hören Musik und finden den _____ wirklich schön.

Kapitel 4

A. Richtig oder falsch? You will hear eight statements based on the **Lesestück** "Studenten in der Bundesrepublik." Check **Richtig** if the statement is correct. Check **Falsch** if it is incorrect.

Richtig	Falsch		Richtig	Falsch		Richtig	Falsch
1._____	_____	4._____	_____	7._____	_____
2._____	_____	5._____	_____	8._____	_____
3._____	_____	6._____	_____	

B. Der richtige Ort°. You will hear six questions concerning the location of certain activities. For each question you will hear two possible answers. Check the letter of the correct answer. | *the right place*

1. a. _____   b. _____   4. a. _____   b. _____
2. a. _____   b. _____   5. a. _____   b. _____
3. a. _____   b. _____   6. a. _____   b. _____

C. Die richtige Entgegnung°. You will hear five questions which might begin a conversation. In your lab manual are two possible responses to each question. Check the reply that makes sense. | *response*

1. _____ a. Nein, ich muß in die Bibliothek.
   _____ b. Ich mache Physik als Hauptfach.
2. _____ a. Mein Referat ist endlich fertig.
   _____ b. Nächstes Semester mache ich Examen.
3. _____ a. Anglistik und Sport. Und du?
   _____ b. Ich muß in acht Semestern fertig werden.
4. _____ a. Ich muß noch zwei Semester studieren.
   _____ b. Nächste Woche muß ich ein Referat schreiben.
5. _____ a. Ja, natürlich, gern.
   _____ b. Ich studiere Musik und Sport.

D. Das richtige Wort. You will hear ten words. Check the word in each printed pair that you hear pronounced.

1. _____ Mutter   _____ Butter   6. _____ gehen   _____ sehen
2. _____ sollen   _____ wollen   7. _____ Beispiel   _____ Bleistift
3. _____ müssen   _____ wissen   8. _____ können   _____ kennen
4. _____ schreiben _____ bleiben   9. _____ Fach   _____ Fisch
5. _____ reich   _____ leicht   10. _____ lesen   _____ essen

E. Eine deutsche Studentin. You will hear a short paragraph about a German student named Dagmar, her studies, and her activities. Listen, then check the correct answers to the questions printed in your lab manual. You will hear the story twice.

1. Was studiert Dagmar?

    _____ a. Sie studiert Physik.

    _____ b. Sie studiert in Marburg.

    _____ c. Sie studiert Germanistik und Geschichte.

2. Warum studiert sie nicht Medizin?

    _____ a. Sie findet es nicht interessant.

    _____ b. Ihr Abitur war nicht gut.

    _____ c. Es gibt keinen Numerus clausus in Medizin.

3. Was macht sie dieses Semester?

    _____ a. Sie schreibt viele Klausuren.

    _____ b. Sie leiht Michael ihre Notizen.

    _____ c. Sie schreibt ein Referat.

4. Wo arbeitet Dagmar für die Klausuren?

    _____ a. Im Seminar.

    _____ b. Im Café.

    _____ c. Sie geht in die Bibliothek.

5. Was kann Dagmar nicht oft tun?

    _____ a. In ein Café gehen und ihre Freunde sehen.

    _____ b. Ins Kino gehen.

    _____ c. Einkaufen gehen.

Kapitel 5

A. Richtig oder falsch? You will hear eight statements based on the **Lesestück** "Österreich."
Check **Richtig** if the statement is correct. Check **Falsch** if it is incorrect.

	Richtig	**Falsch**		**Richtig**	**Falsch**
1.	_____	_____	5.	_____	_____
2.	_____	_____	6.	_____	_____
3.	_____	_____	7.	_____	_____
4.	_____	_____	8.	_____	_____

B. Ist das logisch? You will hear eight pairs of questions and responses. If the response is a
logical reply to the question, check **Logisch.** If the response is not logical, check **Unlogisch.**

	Logisch	**Unlogisch**		**Logisch**	**Unlogisch**
1.	_____	_____	5.	_____	_____
2.	_____	_____	6.	_____	_____
3.	_____	_____	7.	_____	_____
4.	_____	_____	8.	_____	_____

C. Die richtige Wortbedeutung°. You will hear seven statements.
For each statement, you will see two words printed in your lab manual.
Indicate to which of the two words the recorded statement refers.

° the correct meaning

➤+ _____ Auto   ✓ Rad

1. _____ Bern   _____ Wien
2. _____ Ferien   _____ Alpen
3. _____ Paß   _____ Flüchtling
4. _____ wandern   _____ erscheinen
5. _____ Beamte   _____ Auto
6. _____ fliegen   _____ zu Fuß gehen
7. _____ vor kurzem   _____ morgen

D. Ein Interview. A journalist, Frau Berger, is conducting interviews about the traveling
habits of Germans. You will hear one of the interviews. Listen, and then check the correct
answers to the questions printed in your lab manual. You will hear the interview twice.

1. Welches Land ist Ferienland Nummer 1 für die Deutschen?
   _____ a. Die Schweiz.
   _____ b. Österreich.
   _____ c. Dänemark.
2. Warum fahren die Deutschen gern nach Österreich?
   _____ a. In Österreich scheint immer die Sonne.
   _____ b. In Österreich ist das Essen teuer.
   _____ c. Österreich ist ein sehr schönes Land.

3. Wie ist die Reise von der Bundesrepublik nach Österreich?

_____ a. Viele Leute fahren mit dem Motorrad nach Österreich.

_____ b. Man muß sehr lange mit dem Zug fahren.

_____ c. Man braucht nicht lange zu fahren.

4. Was machen die Deutschen, wenn sie nach Österreich fahren?

_____ a. Sie wandern und schwimmen.

_____ b. Sie fahren viel mit dem Rad.

_____ c. Sie spielen Tennis.

5. Wohin fährt Herr Kaiser in den Ferien?

_____ a. Er fährt nach Österreich.

_____ b. Er fliegt nach Dänemark.

_____ c. Er fährt mit einem Freund in die Schweiz.

6. Wo schlafen die Freunde, wenn das Wetter gut ist?

_____ a. Bei Freunden.

_____ b. Im Auto.

_____ c. Sie zelten.

Kapitel 6

A. Richtig oder falsch? You will hear ten statements based on the **Lesestück** "Natürlich."
Check **Richtig** if the statement is correct. Check **Falsch** if it is incorrect. You will hear one new
word:

Kur   *spa*

	Richtig	Falsch		Richtig	Falsch
1.	_____	_____	6.	_____	_____
2.	_____	_____	7.	_____	_____
3.	_____	_____	8.	_____	_____
4.	_____	_____	9.	_____	_____
5.	_____	_____	10.	_____	_____

B. Das Gegenteil°. You will hear five questions containing an | *the opposite*
adjective or an adverb. Complete the answer printed in your lab
manual by checking the antonym of the adjective or adverb you hear.

➤ Nein, er ist ...   ✓ a. kalt   _____ b. gerade

1. Nein, er hat ... Geld.   _____ a. wenig   _____ b. einige
2. Nein, sie war ...   _____ a. wichtig _____ b. schwer
3. Nein, es ist ...   _____ a. teuer   _____ b. einfach
4. Nein, ich gehe ... nach Hause.   _____ a. nie   _____ b. früh
5. Nein, sie ist ...   _____ a. gesund   _____ b. genau

C. Diktat. Tanja and Karla are packing for a trip to Hamburg. Complete their conversation by
filling in the blanks with the words you hear on the tape. You will hear the conversation twice.

Tanja: Glaubst du, wir brauchen sehr warme _____, Karla?

Karla: Nö, ich glaube nicht. Eine _____ und der _____
sind bestimmt genug.

Tanja: _____. Du, _____ du mir deine rote
_____? Die _____ gut _____ zu meinem
schwarzen _____.

Karla: Ja, ja. Was _____ du—soll ich meinen grünen
_____ _____?

Tanja: Nein, bitte nicht!

Karla: Also gut. Aber den grünen _____ ich.

Tanja: Und _____ deine _____ auch nicht!

D. Im Restaurant. Anita and Paul are in a restaurant. They are looking at the menu and deciding what they want to eat. Listen to their conversation, then check the correct answers to the questions printed in your lab manual. You will hear the conversation twice. You will hear one new word:

Flasche   *bottle*

1. Was ißt Anita?
    _____ a. Fisch und Gemüse.
    _____ b. Kuchen.
    _____ c. Brot und Käse.
2. Wie sind die Steaks hier?
    _____ a. Nicht besonders gut.
    _____ b. Leider sehr klein.
    _____ c. Nicht schlecht und ziemlich groß.
3. Hat Paul Hunger?
    _____ a. Nein, er hat keinen Hunger.
    _____ b. Er hat wirklich großen Hunger.
    _____ c. Nein, er hat nur Durst.
4. Wie findet Anita die Schokoladencreme?
    _____ a. Sie weiß nicht.
    _____ b. Nicht besonders gut.
    _____ c. Sie findet, die schmeckt phantastisch.
5. Was trinken die beiden?
    _____ a. Mineralwasser.
    _____ b. Erst Bier, dann Wein.
    _____ c. Cola.

Kapitel 7

A. Richtig oder falsch? You will hear eight statements based on the **Lesestück** "Typisch deutsch? Typisch amerikanisch?" Check **Richtig** if the statement is correct. Check **Falsch** if it is incorrect.

	Richtig	Falsch		Richtig	Falsch
1.	_____	_____	5.	_____	_____
2.	_____	_____	6.	_____	_____
3.	_____	_____	7.	_____	_____
4.	_____	_____	8.	_____	_____

B. Ist das logisch? You will hear eight pairs of questions and responses. If the response is a logical reply to the question, check **Logisch.** If the response is not logical, check **Unlogisch.**

	Logisch	Unlogisch		Logisch	Unlogisch
1.	_____	_____	5.	_____	_____
2.	_____	_____	6.	_____	_____
3.	_____	_____	7.	_____	_____
4.	_____	_____	8.	_____	_____

C. Der richtige Ort°. You will hear six questions about locations. Check the letter of the correct answers. | *place*

1. a. _____	b. _____	4. a. _____	b. _____		
2. a. _____	b. _____	5. a. _____	b. _____		
3. a. _____	b. _____	6. a. _____	b. _____		

D. Erlebnisse° in Deutschland. Thomas, an American student, takes | *experiences*
his first trip to Germany. He sees many things that are quite different
from what he is used to in the U.S. You will hear some of his impressions.
Listen, then check the correct answers to the questions printed in your lab
manual. A question may have more than one correct answer. You will hear
the text twice. You will hear one new word:

Balkon   *balcony*

1. Wo wohnt Thomas in Deutschland?
   _____ a. In einem Studentenheim.
   _____ b. Bei einer Gastfamilie.
   _____ c. In München.
2. Was macht Frau Schneider?
   _____ a. Sie geht jeden Tag in die Bibliothek.
   _____ b. Sie arbeitet an den Blumen auf dem Balkon.
   _____ c. Sie arbeitet am Flughafen.

3. Wie ißt man in Deutschland?

_____ a. Man benutzt Messer und Gabel.

_____ b. Man hat die Hände unter dem Tisch.

_____ c. Man legt die Hände auf den Tisch.

4. Was gibt es im Biergarten?

_____ a. Es gibt große Gläser.

_____ b. Es gibt sehr gutes Essen.

_____ c. Es gibt Blumen und alte Bäume.

5. Was erzählt Thomas über das deutsche Bier?

_____ a. Es schmeckt ziemlich bitter.

_____ b. Die Deutschen trinken es sehr gern.

_____ c. Es ist sehr teuer.

6. Welche Leute kennt Thomas schon?

_____ a. Er kennt nur Familie Schneider.

_____ b. Er hat schon sehr viele Freunde.

_____ c. Er hat schon ein paar Bekannte.

Kapitel 8

A. Richtig oder falsch? You will hear eight statements based on the **Lesestück** "Türen." Check **Richtig** if the statement is correct. Check **Falsch** if it is incorrect.

	Richtig	Falsch		Richtig	Falsch
1.	_____	_____	5.	_____	_____
2.	_____	_____	6.	_____	_____
3.	_____	_____	7.	_____	_____
4.	_____	_____	8.	_____	_____

B. Entgegnungen°. You will hear seven questions which might begin a conversation. Each has two possible responses. Check the response that makes sense.

responses

1. _____ a. Ich habe einen neuen Kassettenrecorder.

   _____ b. Ja, gern. Soll ich etwas mitbringen?

2. _____ a. Einen Plattenspieler.

   _____ b. Ja, ich komme um sieben.

3. _____ a. Gute Idee, vielleicht etwas zu essen.

   _____ b. Ich mache die Küche sauber.

4. _____ a. Das ist ja prima!

   _____ b. Kannst du bitte abtrocknen und aufräumen?

5. _____ a. Wir haben die ganze Zeit getanzt.

   _____ b. Ich hab' leider keine Zeit.

6. _____ a. Ein paar Flaschen Cola.

   _____ b. Ja, natürlich, gern.

7. _____ a. O je, wie es hier aussieht!

   _____ b. Ja bitte, kannst du vielleicht abwaschen?

C. Die gleiche° Bedeutung°. You will hear five pairs of sentences. If the meaning of both sentences is the same, check **Gleich.** If their meaning is different, check **Nicht gleich.**

same / meaning

	Gleich	Nicht gleich		Gleich	Nicht gleich
➤	✓	_____			
1.	_____	_____	4.	_____	_____
2.	_____	_____	5.	_____	_____
3.	_____	_____			

D. Das Haus. You will hear eight sentences concerning the rooms of a house. Check **Richtig** if the statement is correct. Check **Falsch** if it is incorrect.

	Richtig	Falsch		Richtig	Falsch
1.	_____	_____	5.	_____	_____
2.	_____	_____	6.	_____	_____
3.	_____	_____	7.	_____	_____
4.	_____	_____	8.	_____	_____

E. Ein Telefongespräch. Gabi has moved into a new apartment. An old friend telephones her. Listen to their conversation, then check the correct answers to the questions printed in your lab manual. You will hear the conversation twice.

1. Warum ruft Fred bei Gabi an?

   _____ a. Er will sie besuchen.

   _____ b. Er hört, sie hat eine neue Wohnung.

2. Wieviel Zimmer hat Gabis Wohnung?

   _____ a. 6 Zimmer.

   _____ b. 3 Zimmer, Küche und Bad.

3. Was findet Gabi am besten an der Wohnung?

   _____ a. Das große Badezimmer.

   _____ b. Den Balkon.

4. Was denkt Fred über Gabis Miete?

   _____ a. Er findet sie ziemlich teuer.

   _____ b. Er denkt, daß sie recht billig ist.

5. Wann kann Fred Gabis Wohnung sehen?

   _____ a. Heute abend.

   _____ b. Am Samstag, auf der Party.

6. Was macht Gabi, wenn am Samstag schönes Wetter ist?

   _____ a. Sie geht Bücherregale kaufen.

   _____ b. Sie macht die Party auf dem Balkon.

Kapitel 9

A. Richtig oder falsch? You will hear eight statements based on the **Lesestück** "Die Schweiz." Check **Richtig** if the statement is correct. Check **Falsch** if it is incorrect.

Richtig	**Falsch**		**Richtig**	**Falsch**
1. _____	_____	5. _____	_____
2. _____	_____	6. _____	_____
3. _____	_____	7. _____	_____
4. _____	_____	8. _____	_____

B. Entgegnungen°. You will hear five statements or questions about being ill. Check the answer that makes the most sense. | *responses*

1. _____ a. Schade.

_____ b. Du tust mir leid.

_____ c. Nein, ich bin erkältet.

2. _____ a. Ich putze mir morgens die Zähne.

_____ b. Ich fühle mich schwächer als gestern.

_____ c. Ach, wie dumm!

3. _____ a. Du hast recht, sonst kann ich nächste Woche nicht Ski laufen.

_____ b. Hoffentlich bekomme ich diesen Herbst keine Erkältung!

_____ c. Fühlst du dich auch elend?

4. _____ a. Das ist ja toll!

_____ b. Ach, schade!

_____ c. Geh doch zum Zahnarzt!

5. _____ a. Nein, ich glaube nicht.

_____ b. Morgen gehe ich Ski laufen.

_____ c. Nein, ich huste nicht.

C. Körperteile. You will hear five sentences describing parts of the body. Check the correct answer.

1. _____ a. Hände   _____ b. Füße
2. _____ a. Ohren   _____ b. Augen
3. _____ a. Hals   _____ b. Nase
4. _____ a. Zähne   _____ b. Beine
5. _____ a. Finger   _____ b. Haare

D. Ein Interview. Herr Gruber, a journalist, is trying to find out what the Swiss think about their standard of living and the environment. You will hear his interview with a young woman, Frau Beck. Listen, then check the correct answers to the questions printed in your lab manual. A question may have more than one correct answer. You will hear the interview twice. You will hear the following new words:

Lebensstandard	*standard of living*
Chemikalien	*chemicals*
⌐paren	*to save, conserve*
Energie	*energy*
Licht	*light*

1. Wie findet Frau Beck den Lebensstandard in der Schweiz?
   _____ a. Der Lebensstandard ist relativ hoch.
   _____ b. Es gibt sehr viele arme Menschen.
   _____ c. Vieles ist billiger geworden.
2. Führen die Leute jetzt ein einfacheres Leben?
   _____ a. Ja, viele haben keine Waschmaschine und keinen Kühlschrank.
   _____ b. Nein, aber sie sind sparsamer° geworden. | *more thrifty*
   _____ c. Ja, nur wenige können sich Fernseher oder Auto kaufen.
3. Warum hat Frau Beck kein Auto?
   _____ a. Sie braucht es nicht.
   _____ b. Sie kann es sich nicht kaufen.
   _____ c. Sie fährt immer mit dem Rad oder mit dem Zug.
4. Was denken die Schweizer über die Umweltprobleme?
   _____ a. Sie denken wenig daran und tun nichts.
   _____ b. Sie sehen sie ziemlich klar und sprechen darüber.
   _____ c. Sie reden nur und tun nichts.
5. Was tun die Schweizer für die Umwelt?
   _____ a. Sie machen viel Recycling.
   _____ b. Sie fahren mehr mit dem Fahrrad.
   _____ c. Sie versuchen, weniger Chemikalien zu benutzen.
6. Wie sparen sie Energie?
   _____ a. Sie haben kalte Häuser.
   _____ b. Sie sparen am elektrischen Licht.
   _____ c. Sie bauen neue Häuser so, daß sie besser warm bleiben.

Kapitel 10

A. Richtig oder falsch? You will hear eight statements based on the **Lesestück** "Frauen in der Bundesrepublik." Check **Richtig** if the statement is correct. Check **Falsch** if it is incorrect.

	Richtig	Falsch		Richtig	Falsch
1.	_____	_____	5.	_____	_____
2.	_____	_____	6.	_____	_____
3.	_____	_____	7.	_____	_____
4.	_____	_____	8.	_____	_____

B. Ist das logisch? You will hear six short conversational exchanges. If the response is a logical reply to the question or statement, check **Logisch**. If the response is not logical, check **Unlogisch**.

	Logisch	Unlogisch		Logisch	Unlogisch
1.	_____	_____	4.	_____	_____
2.	_____	_____	5.	_____	_____
3.	_____	_____	6.	_____	_____

C. Die richtige Wortbedeutung. You will hear eight statements. For each statement, you will see two words or phrases printed in your lab manual. Check the word to which the recorded statement refers.

1. _____ Briefe _____ Bücher
2. _____ Kollegin _____ Musikerin
3. _____ samstags . _____ in der Nacht
4. _____ Programmierer _____ Lehrer
5. _____ beim Zahnarzt _____ auf der Bank
6. _____ Vorurteile _____ Fremdsprachen
7. _____ Geschirrspüler _____ Waschmaschine
8. _____ Schreibmaschine _____ Möbelstück

D. Ein Gespräch. Listen to the following conversation between two women friends who haven't seen each other for a while. Then check the correct answers to the questions printed in your lab manual. You will hear the dialogue twice. You will hear two new words:

Gratuliere!   *congratulations*
langweilig   *boring*

1. Welchen Beruf hat Renate Bär?
   _____ a. Programmiererin.
   _____ b. Personalchefin.
2. Warum gefällt ihr der neue Job?
   _____ a. Sie kommt viel mit Menschen zusammen.
   _____ b. Sie arbeitet gern mit dem Computer.

3. Welches Problem hat sie in ihrem neuen Job?

_____ a. Sie verdient nicht gut.

_____ b. Einige Männer in der Firma haben Vorurteile gegen sie.

4. Wo arbeitet Angela Kurz?

_____ a. In einer kleinen Firma.

_____ b. In einer Schule.

5. Wie ist die Atmosphäre an Angelas Arbeitsplatz?

_____ a. Ruhig und freundlich.

_____ b. Unfreundlich.

6. Was gefällt Angela Kurz an ihrem Beruf?

_____ a. Die meisten ihrer Kollegen sind Frauen.

_____ b. Sie arbeitet gern mit jungen Leuten.

Kapitel 11

A. Richtig oder falsch? You will hear eight statements based on the **Lesestück** "Freizeit." Check **Richtig** if the statement is correct. Check **Falsch** if it is incorrect.

	Richtig	Falsch		Richtig	Falsch
1.	_____	_____	5.	_____	_____
2.	_____	_____	6.	_____	_____
3.	_____	_____	7.	_____	_____
4.	_____	_____	8.	_____	_____

B. Ist das logisch? You will hear eight pairs of questions and answers. If the response is a logical reply to the question, check **Logisch**. If the response is not logical, check **Unlogisch**.

	Logisch	Unlogisch		Logisch	Unlogisch		Logisch	Unlogisch
1.	_____	_____	4.	_____	_____	7.	_____	_____
2.	_____	_____	5.	_____	_____	8.	_____	_____
3.	_____	_____	6.	_____	_____			

C. Die gleiche Bedeutung. You will hear six pairs of sentences. If the meaning of both sentences is the same, check **Gleich**. If their meaning is different, check **Nicht gleich.**

	Gleich	Nicht gleich		Gleich	Nicht gleich
1.	_____	_____	4.	_____	_____
2.	_____	_____	5.	_____	_____
3.	_____	_____	6.	_____	_____

D. Pläne fürs Wochenende. Karla and Bernd are talking about their plans for the weekend. Listen to their conversation, then check the correct answers to the questions printed in your lab manual. You will hear the dialogue twice. You will hear one new word:

Jugendherberge   *youth hostel*

1. Was wollen Bernd und seine Freunde am Wochenende machen?
   _____ a. Eine Radtour.
   _____ b. Eine Bergwanderung.
2. Wie lange wollen sie bleiben?
   _____ a. Zwei Tage.
   _____ b. Eine Woche.
3. Wo wollen sie schlafen?
   _____ a. Im Hotel.
   _____ b. In der Jugendherberge.
4. Was sind Karlas Pläne fürs Wochenende?
   _____ a. Sie will auf einem Studentenfest spielen.
   _____ b. Sie will tanzen gehen.
5. Ändert sie ihre Pläne?
   _____ a. Nein, sie spielt lieber Musik.
   _____ b. Ja, Bernds Bruder spielt für sie.

6. Spielt die Musikgruppe umsonst°? | *gratis*

_____ a. Ja, das machen sie gern.

_____ b. Nein, jeder bekommt 50 DM.

7. Was soll Karla mitbringen?

_____ a. Ihre Gitarre.

_____ b. Gute Schuhe und etwas gegen Regen.

Kapitel 12

A. Richtig oder falsch? You will hear seven statements based on the **Lesestück** "Zur Wirtschaft der Bundesrepublik." Check **Richtig** if the statement is correct. Check **Falsch** if it is incorrect.

	Richtig	Falsch		Richtig	Falsch
1.	_____	_____	5.	_____	_____
2.	_____	_____	6.	_____	_____
3.	_____	_____	7.	_____	_____
4.	_____	_____			

B. Entgegnungen°. You will hear six questions which might begin a conver-   *responses*
sation. In your lab manual you will see three possible responses to each question.
Check the reply that makes sense.

1. _____ a. Tut mir leid, sie ist heute nicht da.

   _____ b. Ich hoffe, Sie hatten eine gute Reise.

   _____ c. Sie war ein Jahr in den USA.

2. _____ a. Ja, gehen Sie bitte gleich hinein!

   _____ b. Ja, ich habe drei Jahre in Frankreich gearbeitet.

   _____ c. Ich kenne zwei Programmiersprachen.

3. _____ a. Ja bitte, er erwartet Sie schon.

   _____ b. Ich habe einige Fragen.

   _____ c. Nein, leider nicht.

4. _____ a. Ja, ich bin mit dem Zug gefahren.

   _____ b. Nein, ich habe keine Schreibmaschine.

   _____ c. Ja, ich habe schon etwas Erfahrung damit.

5. _____ a. Ich möchte bei einer Exportfirma arbeiten.

   _____ b. Ich glaube ja.

   _____ c. Tut mir leid. Sie ist im Moment beschäftigt.

6. _____ a. Nein, Ihre Preise sind zu hoch.

   _____ b. O ja, die Arbeit muß interessant sein.

   _____ c. Nein, sie telefoniert gerade.

C. Die gleiche Bedeutung. You will hear seven sentences. For each one, you will see an in-
complete sentence printed in your lab manual. Check the word or phrase that completes the
printed sentence with a meaning similar to the recorded one.

1. Sie hat ...   _____ a. Urlaub   _____ b. einen Termin

2. Ich bin nur ... müde.   _____ a. ein bißchen   _____ b. einzeln

3. Sie wohnen ...   _____ a. in einer Wohnung   _____ b. auf dem Lande

4. Sie sind ...   _____ a. allgemein   _____ b. niedrig

5. Er geht ... spazieren.   _____ a. selten   _____ b. immer

6. Da habe ich ...   _____ a. keinen Streß   _____ b. einen Unfall

7. Ich habe ihn ...   _____ a. angerufen   _____ b. erwartet

D. Die richtige Wortbedeutung. You will hear six statements. For each statement, you will see two words printed in your lab manual. Check the word to which the recorded statement refers.

1. _____ Freizeit _____ Zukunft
2. _____ Kauffrau _____ Kundin
3. _____ beschäftigen _____ zahlen
4. _____ Gewerkschaft _____ Mitglied
5. _____ Grenze _____ Hof
6. _____ Streiks _____ Handel

E. Zwei Gespräche. You will hear two short dialogues. Listen, then read the statements printed in your lab manual. Check **Richtig** if the statement is correct, **Falsch** if it is incorrect, or **Man weiß es nicht** if the information was not in the dialogue. You will hear each dialogue twice.

	Richtig	Falsch	Man weiß es nicht
1. Frau Schulze erwartet Herrn Meier.	_____	_____	_____
2. Frau Schulze kann ihn heute nicht sehen.	_____	_____	_____
3. Die Sekretärin will Frau Schulze fragen, ob sie Zeit hat.	_____	_____	_____
4. Frau Schulze hat jetzt einen Termin.	_____	_____	_____
1. Frau Schulze findet Herrn Meiers Sachen billig.	_____	_____	_____
2. Sie hat aber viele Fragen wegen der Qualität.	_____	_____	_____
3. Frau Schulze ruft Herrn Meier am Montag an.	_____	_____	_____
4. Sie wird die Sachen von Herrn Meier kaufen.	_____	_____	_____

Kapitel 13

A. Richtig oder falsch?   You will hear ten statements based on the **Lesestück** "Eindrücke aus der DDR." Check **Richtig** if the statement is correct. Check **Falsch** if it is incorrect.

	Richtig	Falsch		Richtig	Falsch
1.	_____	_____	6.	_____	_____
2.	_____	_____	7.	_____	_____
3.	_____	_____	8.	_____	_____
4.	_____	_____	9.	_____	_____
5.	_____	_____	10.	_____	_____

B. Ist das logisch?   You will hear eight short conversational exchanges. If the response is a logical reply, check **Logisch.** If the response is not logical, check **Unlogisch.**

	Logisch	Unlogisch		Logisch	Unlogisch		Logisch	Unlogisch
1.	_____	_____	4.	_____	_____	7.	_____	_____
2.	_____	_____	5.	_____	_____	8.	_____	_____
3.	_____	_____	6.	_____	_____			

C. Die gleiche Bedeutung.   You will hear six pairs of sentences. If the meaning of both sentences is the same, check **Gleich.** If their meaning is different, check **Nicht gleich.**

	Gleich	Nicht gleich		Gleich	Nicht gleich
1.	_____	_____	4.	_____	_____
2.	_____	_____	5.	_____	_____
3.	_____	_____	6.	_____	_____

D. Ein Gespräch.   You will hear a short conversation between Georg and Ursel. Listen, then check the correct answers to the questions printed in your lab manual. You will hear their conversation twice.

1. Warum ist Georg so müde?
    _____ a. Er war gestern abend in der Oper.
    _____ b. Er jobbt auf dem Theaterfestival.
2. Was für eine Arbeit hat Georg?
    _____ a. Er macht Musik.
    _____ b. Er macht Reklame für das Theater.
3. Warum macht Georg diese Arbeit?
    _____ a. Alles, was mit dem Theater zu tun hat, interessiert ihn.
    _____ b. Weil er gut verdient.
4. Was macht Georg meistens mit den Freikarten?
    _____ a. Er benutzt sie selbst.
    _____ b. Er gibt sie Freunden.

5. Warum geht Ursel mit ins Theater?

   _____ a. Sie hat heute abend nichts anderes zu tun.

   _____ b. Den *Faust* fand sie sehr interessant, als sie ihn in der Schule las.

6. Wo wollen sie sich treffen?

   _____ a. Georg holt Ursel ab.

   _____ b. Sie treffen sich am Theater.

Kapitel 14

A. Richtig oder falsch? You will hear ten statements based on the **Lesestück** "Ausländische Arbeitnehmer." Check **Richtig** if the statement is correct. Check **Falsch** if it is incorrect.

	Richtig	Falsch		Richtig	Falsch
1.	_____	_____	6.	_____	_____
2.	_____	_____	7.	_____	_____
3.	_____	_____	8.	_____	_____
4.	_____	_____	9.	_____	_____
5.	_____	_____	10.	_____	_____

B. Ist das logisch? You will hear eight short conversational exchanges. If the response is a logical reply, check **Logisch.** If the response is not logical, check **Unlogisch.**

	Logisch	Unlogisch		Logisch	Unlogisch		Logisch	Unlogisch
1.	_____	_____	4.	_____	_____	7.	_____	_____
2.	_____	_____	5.	_____	_____	8.	_____	_____
3.	_____	_____	6.	_____	_____			

C. Der richtige Ort. You will hear six questions about locations. For each question you will hear two possible answers. Check the letter of the correct answer.

1. a. _____ b. _____   4. a. _____ b. _____
2. a. _____ b. _____   5. a. _____ b. _____
3. a. _____ b. _____   6. a. _____ b. _____

D. Ein Interview. Birgit, a staff member of the local **Jugendzeitung,** is interviewing Ali, a Turk who lives in Germany. Listen to their conversation, then check the correct answers to the questions printed in your lab manual. You will hear the interview twice.

1. Wann ist Ali in die Bundesrepublik gekommen?
   _____ a. Als er sehr klein war.
   _____ b. Als er 17 war.
2. Warum ist Ali nach Deutschland gekommen?
   _____ a. Sein Vater fand in der Türkei keine Arbeit.
   _____ b. Er wollte Deutsch lernen.
3. Warum spricht Ali so gut Deutsch?
   _____ a. Er geht auf eine deutsche Schule und hat ein paar deutsche Freunde.
   _____ b. Er spricht mit seinen Eltern oft Deutsch.
4. Was sind Alis Zukunftspläne?
   _____ a. Er will Elektroingenieur sein.
   _____ b. Er will in einem türkischen Laden arbeiten.
5. Was gefällt Ali am türkischen Viertel?
   _____ a. Dort wohnen viele Freunde seiner Eltern.
   _____ b. Dort wird er von den Deutschen in Ruhe° gelassen. | *in peace*

6. Was gefällt ihm nicht am türkischen Viertel?

_____ a. Dort ist es so laut.

_____ b. Er hat nicht genug Kontakt zu Deutschen.

7. Wo möchte Ali später mal leben?

_____ a. Er möchte in die Türkei zurückgehen; dort ist seine Heimat.

_____ b. Er möchte in Deutschland bleiben.

Workbook

Einführung

A. Wie bitte? Supply appropriate questions to complete the following conversation between the secretary and Stephan Meyer.

1. *Sekretär:* _____?
   Stephan: Ich heiße Stephan Meyer.

2. *Sekretär:* _____?
   Stephan: M–E–Y–E–R.

3. *Sekretär:* _____?
   Stephan: 40 21 11.

B. Rechnen°. Write out each of the following math problems. | *arithmetic*

1. 19 + 8 = 27

_____

2. 70 – 1 = 69

_____

3. 5 × 17 = 85

_____

4. 1.000 ÷ 10 = 100

_____

C. Wochentage. Answer each question by writing the appropriate day or days of the week in German.

1. Which two days constitute the weekend? _____ und _____

2. Which day is the middle of the week? _____

3. The German word for *moon* is **Mond;** which day is named after the moon? _____

4. **Freyia** was the Germanic goddess of love; which day is named after her? _____

5. The Germanic god of thunder was **Donar;** which day is named after him? _____

D. Welcher Artikel? Give the definite article for each of the following nouns.

➥ *die* Frau

1. _____ Papier   5. _____ Sekretärin
2. _____ Bleistift   6. _____ Heft
3. _____ Woche   7. _____ Tag
4. _____ Wort   8. _____ Telefon

E. Wie alt ist...? First complete each question by providing the pictured noun and its definite article. Then write out the cued age in years in a full sentence, replacing the noun with the appropriate pronoun.

➥ Wie alt ist *der Student?* (18)
Er ist achtzehn Jahre alt.

1. Wie alt ist _____? (212)

_____

_____

2. Wie alt ist _____? (54)

_____

_____

3. Wie alt ist _____? (3)

_____

_____

4. Wie alt ist _____? (106)

_____

_____

5. Wie alt ist _____? (7)

_____

_____

6. Wie alt ist _____? (21)

_____

_____

7. Wie alt ist _____? (60)

_____

_____

8. Wie alt ist _____? (2)

_____

_____

F. Welche Farben? Complete the bilingual color guide for these road signs.

blue _____   red _____   yellow _____

white _____   black _____   green _____

G. Landeskunde°. Provide brief responses in English. | *culture*

1. Compare the academic year at a German university with the academic year at your school.

_____

_____

2. Compare what you say when you answer the phone at home with what a German speaker would say.

_____

_____

H. Wie? Was? Express the following questions in German. Then answer each question with a complete sentence.

1. How old are you?

_____

_____

2. What day is today?

_____

_____

3. What color is the workbook°? | *das Übungs-*
                                                    buch

_____

_____

4. Your name is Kim, isn't it?

_____

_____

Einführung 35

I. Das ideale Zimmer. You've been asked to prepare a color sketch of an ideal dorm room for a publicity brochure. Write five sentences with nouns and various modifiers (colors, size, age) to describe the room: **Das Zimmer ist ..., Das Fenster ist ...**

_____

_____

_____

_____

J. Sie haben das Wort. Give the following information about yourself.

1. Wie heißen Sie?

_____

2. Wie ist Ihre Adresse?

_____

3. Wie ist Ihre Telefonnummer?

_____

Kapitel 1

A. Frau...? Mrs. Gärtner runs into Mrs. Schmidt on the street but doesn't remember her name. Complete their conversation in a logical manner.

Frau Schmidt: _____

Frau Gärtner: Guten Abend, Frau... Frau...?

Frau Schmidt: _____

Frau Gärtner: Ach, ja! Frau Schmidt! Wie geht es Ihnen, Frau Schmidt?

Frau Schmidt: _____

Frau Gärtner: Danke, ganz gut.

B. Gehen wir tanzen? Complete the conversation between Klaus and Erika.

Klaus: Tag Erika!

Erika: _____

Klaus: Was machst du heute nachmittag?

Erika: _____

Klaus: Gehst du heute abend mit mir tanzen?

Erika: _____

C. Vokabeln. Complete each sentence with a word chosen from the list below.

du, ich, machen, Professor Schumacher, schlecht, wie

1. _____ geht es Ihnen?

2. Es geht Frau Müller _____.

3. _____ bin sehr müde.

4. Arbeitest _____ mit Karin?

5. _____ sagt: „Guten Abend."

6. Wir _____ das heute abend.

D. Wann? While staying in Luzern, you plan an excursion on the lake. Use the steamer schedule to answer the questions, spelling out the times. For the first answer, use conversational German (Method 1); for the second answer, use the official 24-hour clock (Method 2).

Luzern	(ab) dp pt	9.30
WEGGIS X	(an) ar	10.09
	(ab) dp pt	10.32
KEHRSITEN X	(an) ar	10.50
	(ab) dp pt	11.00
ALPNACHSTAD	(an) ar	12.00
	(ab) dp pt	15.10
Luzern	(an) ar	16.45
	ab dp pt	

1. Wann fahren° wir von° Luzern ab?   *fahren...ab: depart / from*

   a. Um _____

   b. Um _____

2. Wann kommen° wir in Weggis an?   *kommen...an: arrive*

   a. Um _____

   b. Um _____

3. Wann fahren wir von Kehrsiten ab?

   a. Um _____

   b. Um _____

4. Wann kommen wir in Luzern an?

   a. Um _____

   b. Um _____

E. Neue Subjekte. Rewrite each sentence, using the cue as a new subject.

1. Ich bin nicht krank. (Professor Braun)

_____

2. Glauben sie das? (ihr)

_____

3. Wie heißen Sie? (du)

_____

4. Sie wandert gern. (wir)

_____

5. Sind Sie auch krank? (du)

_____

6. Ich gehe heute abend ins Kino. (er)

_____

7. Frau Schmidt arbeitet viel. (Hans und Erik)

_____

8. Was machst du heute morgen? (sie, *sg.*)

_____

9. Tanzt Herr Braun gern? (du)

_____

F. Nein, nein. Answer each question in the negative.

➥ Ist das Radio alt?   *Nein, das Radio ist nicht alt.*

1. Ist das Zimmer groß?

_____

2. Glaubt sie das?

_____

3. Arbeitet Fräulein Wagner in Bonn?

_____

4. Glaubst du Mark?

_____

5. Gehst du heute nachmittag ins Kino?

_____

6. Sind Klaus und Michael faul?

_____

7. Spielt ihr gern Basketball?

_____

8. Ist das Frau Kraft?

_____

9. Wandern Gabi und Erika oft?

_____

G. Wer? Was? Wann?   Write specific questions, using the cues provided. Remember that a verb must agree with its subject.

➡ wann / gehen / Thomas / ?   *Wann geht Thomas?*

1. wann / arbeiten / Frau Lange / ?

_____

2. wer/ glauben / das / ?

_____

3. warum / schwimmen / ihr / nicht auch / ?

_____

4. wann / gehen / Sie / ins Kino / ?

_____

5. wie / machen / ich / das / ?

_____

6. was für Musik / hören / du / gern / ?

_____

7. wie alt / sein / Ute und Monika / ?

_____

8. wann / machen / wir / das / ?

_____

9. warum / tanzen / du / nicht / gern / ?

_____

H. Ja und nein. Write a general question to which each of the following sentences would be a logical response.

1. _____

   Nein, ich arbeite heute abend nicht.

2. _____

   Nein, er geht nicht ins Kino.

3. _____

   Nein, sie heißt nicht Monika.

4. _____

   Ja, ihr arbeitet heute abend.

5. _____

   Nein, Lutz glaubt das nicht.

6. _____

   Ja, wir gehen auch schwimmen.

I. Sie, du oder ihr? Use the cues provided to write a question addressed to the person in parentheses, using **du, ihr,** or **Sie** as appropriate.

➤ (Frau Braun) glauben / das / ?   *Glauben Sie das?*

1. (Erika) spielen / oft / Tennis / ?

   _____

2. (Inge und Lutz) gehen / ins Kino / ?

   _____

3. (Herr Wagner) wandern / gern / ?

   _____

4. (Jürgen) treiben / viel / Sport / ?

   _____

5. (Frau Schmidt) hören / das / nicht / ?

   _____

**SIE WISSEN JA SELBST,
WAS GUT ODER SCHLECHT FÜR SIE IST.**

J. Was? Wann? Your Austrian neighbor asks you about your activities. Check the calendar and respond in German using complete sentences with **Ja,...** or with **Nein,...** and the correct activity.

MONDAY	*play volleyball*
TUESDAY	*play chess with Max*
WEDNESDAY	*listen to music*
THURSDAY	*work with Inge*
FRIDAY	*go dancing*
SATURDAY	*go swimming*
SUNDAY	*go to the movies*

➤ *Freitag:* Wir gehen schwimmen, nicht?   *Nein, wir gehen tanzen.*

1. *Dienstag:* Du spielst Schach, nicht?

_____

2. *Donnerstag:* Gehen wir ins Kino?

_____

3. *Montag:* Wir spielen Fußball, nicht?

_____

4. *Mittwoch:* Gehst du heute abend schwimmen?

_____

5. *Samstag:* Spielen wir heute morgen Tennis?

_____

6. *Sonntag:* Du arbeitest heute viel, nicht?

_____

K. Wie sagt man das? Give the German equivalent of each of the following sentences.

1. Petra is working this afternoon.

_____

2. I like to hear music.

_____

3. Do you believe that, Karin?

_____

4. Does Mr. Klein like to play chess?

_____

5. When are they going to the movies?

_____

6. Do you like to hike, Erik and Ute?

_____

7. Are you working today, Ms. Becker?

_____

8. Fritz likes to swim, doesn't he (isn't that so)?

_____

L. Landeskunde. Provide brief responses in English.

1. What are the general guidelines for using **du** and **Sie?**

_____

_____

2. Compare how people in Germany and people in your country participate in competitive sports.

_____

_____

M. Wer sind Sie? You are applying for a job as a counselor at a summer camp. Complete the form below. Use complete sentences for questions 4 to 7.

1. Name: _____

2. Adresse: _____

3. Telefon: _____

4. Was für ein Mensch sind Sie? _____

_____

5. Schwimmen Sie gut? _____

Aktivitäten:

6. Was machen Sie gern? _____

_____

7. Was machen Sie nicht gern? _____

_____

Kapitel 2

A. Wie ist das Wetter? Ms. Weiss and Mr. Dorn are tired of rainy weather, but like many people they never get tired of talking about it. Complete their conversation.

Frau Weiss: Guten Morgen, Herr Dorn!

Herr Dorn: _____!

Frau Weiss: Was für ein Wetter!

Herr Dorn: _____.

Frau Weiss: Ich glaube, es schneit bald.

Herr Dorn: _____.

B. Wo waren Sie? Complete each sentence with the correct form of the simple past tense of **sein.**

1. Wir _____ in Frankreich.

2. _____ das Mädchen in Belgien?

3. Ich _____ in Dänemark.

4. _____ Frau Kohl wieder in der Schweiz?

5. Ihr _____ in Polen, nicht?

6. _____ Sie in Österreich?

7. Wer _____ in Kanada?

8. Du _____ in Spanien, nicht?

C. Adverbien. Rewrite each sentence, beginning with the cued word. Be sure not to delete any of the original words in rewriting the sentences.

1. Das Wetter ist furchtbar. (heute)

_____

2. Das Mädchen geht bestimmt nicht. (jetzt)

_____

3. Es regnet wieder. (morgen)

_____

4. Der Wind ist sehr kalt. (im Winter)

_____

5. Es ist aber schön warm. (im Süden)

_____

6. Ich bleibe in Italien. (vielleicht) *maybe*

_____

D. Wie? Wann?   Answer each question in a complete sentence, using the cues provided.

1. Wie ist das Wetter? (schön)

_____

2. Wann regnet es viel? (im Frühling)

_____

3. Wann schneit es? (im Winter)

_____

4. Wo ist das Wetter anders? (in Österreich)

_____

5. Wieviel Nachbarn hat Österreich? (sieben)

_____

6. Wieviel Nachbarn haben die DDR und die Bundesrepublik? (neun)

_____

E. Wo ist das Subjekt?   In each sentence underline the subject once. Some of the sentences contain a predicate noun. Underline each predicate noun twice.

1. Bonn ist die Hauptstadt der Bundesrepublik.

2. Für Amerikaner ist Deutschland sehr klein. *pred adj*

3. Heute ist es aber heiß.

4. Die Deutschen sagen das.

5. In Deutschland ist das Wetter anders.

6. Die Frau da ist Amerikanerin, nicht?

7. Sie heißt Carol Jones. *pred noun prop name*

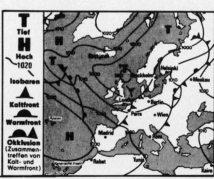

DAS WETTER

DIE LAGE

Das Sturmtief über der Nordsee schwächt sich langsam ab und zieht nach Skandinavien. Auf seiner Rückseite wird frische Meeresluft herangeführt. In einer lebhaften westlichen Strömung überqueren weitere Tiefausläufer in rascher Folge Deutschland. Wetterberuhigung deutet sich erst für's Wochenende an.

© 1988 by Houghton Mifflin Company

F. Fragen°. Construct a question from each set of guidelines. | *questions*
Add articles where necessary. Be sure the subject and verb agree.

1. wann / scheinen / Sonne / wieder / ?

_____

2. warum / regnen / es / so oft / ?

_____

3. wer / finden / Wetter / schön / ?

_____

4. wie / sein / Sommer / in Deutschland / ?

_____

5. was / denken / ihr / ?

_____

6. wo / sein / Winter / warm / ?

_____

7. was / sagen / Nachbarinnen / ?

_____

G. Singular und Plural. Decide whether each word given is singular or plural. Then write it
in the proper column and add the other form.

	Singular	**Plural**
1. die Herren	_____	_____
2. die Kinder	_____	_____
3. der Tag	_____	_____
4. das Wort	_____	_____
5. die Mädchen	_____	_____
6. die Städte	_____	_____
7. der Tisch	_____	_____
8. die Frau	_____	_____
9. das Fenster	_____	_____
10. die Lampe	_____	_____

H. Der, die oder das? Arrange the words according to gender. For those nouns preceded by an asterisk, also give the plural notation.

➤ *Monat *Monat, -e*

*Abend, *Bett, *Bleistift, *Farbe, *Fräulein, Frühling, Herbst, *Karte, *Kino, *Mensch, Musik, Papier, Schnee, Sonne, *Telefon, *Wand, *Woche, *Zimmer

Masculine   **Neuter**   **Feminine**

_____ _____ _____

_____ _____ _____

_____ _____ _____

_____ _____ _____

_____ _____ _____

         _____ _____

I. Nicht oder kein-? Answer each question in the negative, using **nicht** or **kein-** as appropriate. Replace each noun subject with its corresponding pronoun.

➤ Ist der Mann Sekretär?   *Nein, er ist kein Sekretär.*

1. Ist die Professorin Berlinerin? _____

2. Sind die Mädchen Studentinnen? _____

3. Ist Max Winter der Professor? _____

4. Sind die Nachbarn Amerikaner? _____

5. Ist der Herr Deutscher? _____

6. Ist Frau Weber die Sekretärin? _____

J. Wie sagt man das? Complete each sentence with the German equivalent of the cued word.

1. Da liegt _____ Heft. (*my*)

2. Wo sind _____ Bücher, Kai und Markus? (*your*)

3. Ist das _____ Poster? (*Rita's*)

4. Hier ist _____ Lampe. (*her*)

5. Ist das _____ Bleistift, Herr Winter? (*your*)

6. Ist das auch _____ Kuli? (*his*)

K. Ja und nein. Answer each question in the affirmative, replacing the noun phrase with its corresponding demonstrative pronoun.

➤ Der Staat ist klein, nicht?   Ja, *der ist klein*.

1. Die Schweiz ist sehr schön, nicht?

   Ja, _____

2. Die Städte sind sehr alt, nicht?

   Ja, _____

3. Herr Schneider arbeitet in Bern, nicht?

   Ja, _____

4. Kirstin arbeitet in Luzern, nicht?

   Ja, _____

5. Die Nachbarn bleiben in St. Moritz, nicht?

   Ja, _____

Answer each question in the negative, replacing the noun phrase with its corresponding personal pronoun.

➤ Sagt Maria viel?   Nein, *viel sagt sie nicht*.

1. Scheint die Sonne heute?

   Nein, _____

2. Arbeitet Herr Hofer morgen?

   Nein, _____

3. Ist das Wetter warm?

   Nein, _____

4. Ist der Garten groß?

   Nein, _____

5. Spielen Klaus und Maria gut?

   Nein, _____

L. Landeskunde. Provide brief responses in English.

1. Identify two typical birthday customs in German-speaking countries that are the same as those in your country and two customs that are different.

_____

_____

_____

2. When is **Hochdeutsch** used in German-speaking countries?

_____

_____

M. Sie haben das Wort. Respond appropriately.

Expressing Agreement

1. *Freund/in:* Was für ein Wetter!

   Du: _____

2. *Freund/in:* Ich glaube, es schneit bald.

   Du: _____

Expressing Expectation or Hope

3. *Freund/in:* Morgen scheint die Sonne bestimmt.

   Du: _____

N. Was sagt man? Write a brief conversational exchange appropriate to each of the seasons. Use known vocabulary and structures.

1. _____   2. _____

   _____   _____

   _____   _____

3. _____   4. _____

   _____   _____

   _____   _____

O. Deutsche Städte. Identify the five rivers (**Flüsse**) and fifteen cities marked on the map of the two German states. Refer to the map on the inside cover of your textbook as necessary.

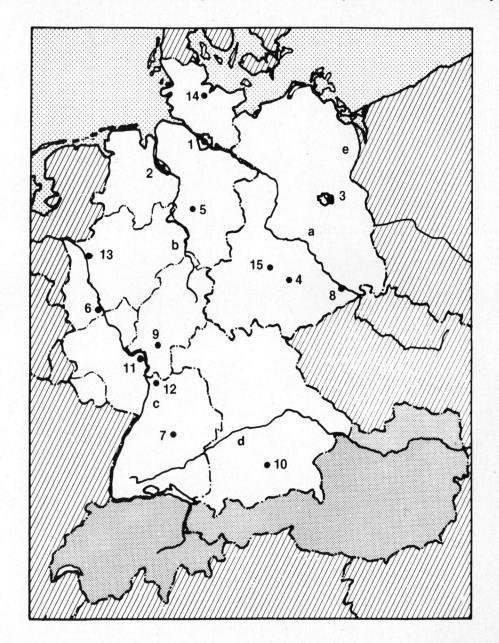

Flüsse	Städte		
a. _____	1. _____	6. _____	11. _____
b. _____	2. _____	7. _____	12. _____
c. _____	3. _____	8. _____	13. _____
d. _____	4. _____	9. _____	14. _____
e. _____	5. _____	10. _____	15. _____

P. Europa. The lists below provide the names and the capital cities of each of the countries numbered on the map. Write the name of the country beside its number, and match the country with its capital.

Belgien, Dänemark, Frankreich, Luxemburg, die Niederlande, Österreich, Polen, die Schweiz, die Tschechoslowakei

Amsterdam, Bern, Brüssel, Kopenhagen, Luxemburg, Paris, Prag, Warschau, Wien

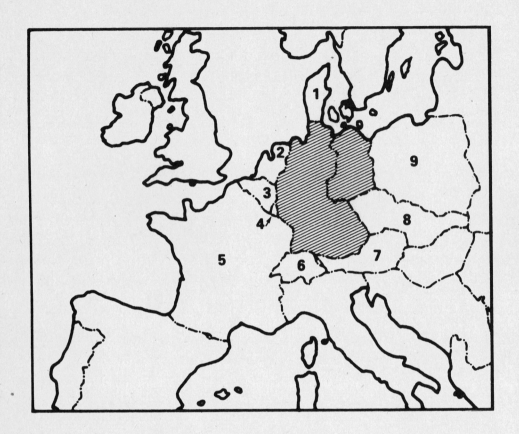

Land	Hauptstadt
1. _____	_____
2. _____	_____
3. _____	_____
4. _____	_____
5. _____	_____
6. _____	_____
7. _____	_____
8. _____	_____
9. _____	_____

Kapitel 3

A. Einkaufen. Complete the conversation between Daniel and Thomas in a logical manner.

1. *Daniel:* Gehst du heute nicht einkaufen?

   Thomas: _____

2. *Daniel:* Gut. Wir brauchen Kaffee.

   Thomas: _____

   Daniel: Ja, Weißbrot und Toastbrot.

3. *Thomas:* Ich gehe dann zu Meier.

   Daniel: _____

B. Was kauft man da? Lore is running errands. Name two things she can buy in each store.

1. Lore geht ins Kaufhaus.   _____   _____

2. Dann geht sie in die Apotheke.   _____   _____

3. Sie geht in den Supermarkt.   _____   _____

4. Dann geht sie zum Metzger.   _____   _____

5. Dann geht sie zum Bäcker.   _____   _____

6. Sie geht auch auf den Markt.   _____   _____

C. Neue Wörter. Form a compound from each pair of nouns. Write the compound with its definite article and give the English equivalent.

	Compound	English Equivalent
1. der Kaffee und das Haus	____ _____	_____
2. die Wand und die Uhr	____ _____	_____
3. die Butter und das Brot	____ _____	_____
4. der Sommer und der Abend	____ _____	_____
5. der Frühling (+ s) und der Tag	____ _____	_____
6. das Haus und die Tür	____ _____	_____
7. der Winter und das Wetter	____ _____	_____
8. der Herbst und der Wind	____ _____	_____

D. Was ißt man gern? Rewrite each sentence, using the cue as the new subject.

1. Nehmt ihr Tee? (du)

_____

Kapitel 3   53

2. Gibst du mir das Brot, bitte? (Sie)

_____

3. Ich finde die Brötchen trocken. (Erika)

_____

4. Frau und Herr Schneider geben Erika den Wein. (Klaus)

_____

5. Essen Sie keinen Fisch? (du)

_____   _____

6. Sie nimmt einen Liter Milch. (ich)

_____

7. Brauchen wir Tee? (du)

_____

8. Gebt ihr Frau Braun nichts? (Renate)

_____

9. Ißt er gern Spaghetti? (ihr)

_____

E. Befehle°. Complete the commands, using the form of the cued verb | *commands*
that corresponds to the person or persons given.

➡ _____ Professor Keller! (Renate und Jürgen / fragen)
    Fragt Professor Keller!

1. _____ nicht so nervös! (Gabi und Frank / sein)

2. _____ mir bitte zwei Pfund Kaffee! (Herr Winter / geben)

3. _____ Tee! (Michael und Sonja / kochen)

4. _____ den Kuchen nicht! (Paul / essen)

5. _____ mir bitte die Adresse! (Frau Klein / geben)

6. _____ doch nett! (Lutz / sein)

7. _____ den Stuhl! (Helga / nehmen)

8. _____ bald wieder! (Frau und Herr Becker / kommen)

F. Auf dem Markt. You are shopping in Bremen's market. Decide how much of each numbered item 1, 2, and 3 you want and compute the cost. Use this information to complete your conversation with the vendors. Then select item #4 or #5 and write a short exchange with the vendor. (Note: **das Stück** = piece or item.)

➤ — Geben Sie mir bitte *ein Pfund Erdbeeren°*! | *strawberries*
— Das macht *zwei Mark fünfzig*.

1. — Geben Sie mir bitte _____

— Das macht _____

2. — Ich nehme _____

— Das macht _____

3. — Geben Sie mir bitte _____

— _____, bitte.

Item 4. or 5. _____

_____

_____

G. Nominativ und Akkusativ. Underline each subject once and each direct object twice.

1. Im Tante-Emma-Laden kennt man Monika und Andrea.

2. Die Amerikanerin versteht Herr Meier nicht.

3. Geben Sie mir bitte ein Pfund!

4. Sie nehmen den Kaffee doch ungemahlen, nicht?

5. Wieviel Gramm Käse braucht sie heute?

6. Wo findet man Tabletten?

7. Frag doch Herrn Müller!

8. Auf dem Markt kaufen wir Blumen, nicht?

9. Die Studentinnen haben bestimmt viele Fragen.

H. Akkusativ. Complete each sentence with the correct form of the word or phrase in parentheses.

1. Für _____ arbeitest du? (wer)

2. Ich arbeite für _____. (Herr Schmidt)

3. Er geht jetzt durch _____. (die Buchhandlung)

4. Kennst du _____ da? (der Junge)

5. _____ fragst du? (wer)

6. Er geht um _____. (sein Haus)

7. Ohne _____ kommen wir nicht! (die Nachbarn)

8. Wir haben _____ besonders gern. (unser Nachbar)

9. Ihr habt also nichts gegen _____? (die Leute)

10. Gibt es heute _____ Kaffee? (kein)

I. Nicht oder kein-? Make each sentence negative, using **kein-** if the noun has an indefinite article or no article, or **nicht** if the noun has a definite article or possessive adjective.

1. Jürgen braucht seine Einkaufstasche. _____

2. Nimmt er das Graubrot? _____

3. Ich koche den Kaffee. _____

4. Wir brauchen Kaffee. _____

5. Gibt es hier Bäckereien? _____

6. Julia kauft einen Kuchen. _____

7. Diane findet die Apotheke. _____

8. Sie kauft Vitamintabletten. _____

J. Bitte nicht. No one wants to lend Rudi a car. Complete each sentence with the accusative pronoun that corresponds to the noun or pronoun in parentheses.

1. Frag _____ bitte nicht! (ich)

2. Frag _____ bitte nicht! (wir)

3. Frag _____ nicht! (Thomas)

4. Frag _____ nicht! (Jan und Inge)

5. Frag _____ nicht! (Frau Lange)

K. *Deutsch heute* **Diät.** Tanja and Erik are thinking about dieting. Prepare a day's menu for them, based on the vocabulary in *Kapitel 3*.

Zum Frühstück: Essen Sie _____ und

_____, aber kein _____!

Zum Mittagessen: Essen Sie _____,

_____ und _____,

aber kein _____ und kein

_____!

Zum Abendessen: Essen Sie _____ und

_____, aber kein

_____!

Trinken° Sie viel _____ oder | *drink*

_____, aber kein _____

_____!

L. Das Picknick. Erika and Anja want to pack a picnic, but make a series of unpleasant discoveries. Express their conversation in German.

Anja: We don't have any cheese.

_____

Erika: Are you going shopping this morning?

_____

Anja: Yes, but I don't have much money.

_____

Erika: Buy the cheese at Neumann's.

_____

Anja: It's better and cheaper there, isn't it?

_____

Erika: We also need rolls.

_____

Anja: Those I'll buy at the bakery. But I don't have money for the wine.

_____

Erika: As always!

_____

M. Landeskunde. Provide brief responses in English.

1. Name three things you would find particulary enjoyable about shopping at an outdoor market in a German-speaking country.

_____

_____

2. State two differences between weekend shopping hours in Germany and in your community.

_____

_____

N. Sie haben das Wort. Respond appropriately to the following statements.

Giving Advice

1. *Freund/in:* Wir haben keine Wurst mehr.
   Du: _____

2. *Freund/in:* Ich brauche ein Buch über Schach.
   Du: _____

Expressing Likes and Dislikes

3. *Freund/in:* Was ißt du gern zum Frühstück?
   Du: _____

4. *Freund/in:* Was machst du abends nicht gern?
   Du: _____

O. Die Party. Turn to the drawing on page 90 of your textbook. Write a conversation for one of the three sets of people. They may talk about the weather, their activities, or food. Be sure to use known vocabulary and structures.

_____

_____

_____

_____

_____

Kapitel 4

A. Mußt du arbeiten? Sabine and Andreas are talking about the work they have to do. Express their conversation in German.

Sabine: Hi Andreas, how are you?

_____

Andreas: Fine. I have to read an article for my report. What are you doing?

_____

_____

Sabine: I have to study for the test.

_____

Andreas: Would you like to work together?

_____

Sabine: Glad to. Afterwards we can go for coffee.

_____

B. Was meinen Sie? Complete the survey by answering the questions for each college major. (For translations, refer to page R-26 of your text.) Use the following scale:

1 = ja, sehr
2 = ja
3 = durchschnittlich (*average*)
4 = eigentlich nicht
5 = gar nicht (*not at all*)

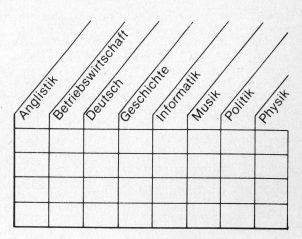

1. Das Hauptfach ist schwer.

2. Das Hauptfach hat großes Prestige.

3. Mit diesem Hauptfach ist es relativ leicht, einen Job zu finden.

4. Das Hauptfach ist interessant.

C. Wer ist denn das? You are showing family photos to a roommate who is far-sighted. First correct the mistaken identifications as you wish. Then supply your own answers concerning professions and nationality.

➤ Ist das deine Kusine?   *Nein, das ist meine Tante.*
  Ist sie Sozialarbeiterin?   *Nein, sie ist Professorin.*

1. Ist das dein Bruder? _____

  Ist er Apotheker? _____

2. Das ist deine Mutter, nicht? _____

  Ist sie Spanierin? _____

3. Sind das deine zwei Vettern? _____

  Sind sie Elektriker? _____

4. Ist das dein Großvater? _____

  Ist er Frankfurter? _____

5. Das ist deine Kusine, nicht? _____

  Was will sie werden? _____

D. Das Examen. People react differently to upcoming major exams. Complete each sentence with the correct form of the verb in parentheses.

1. – _____ du nervös? (werden)

  – Klar. Und ich _____ auch sehr müde. (werden)

2. – _____ du den Studenten da? (sehen)

  – Ja. Der _____ jeden Tag in der Bibliothek. (lesen)

3. – _____ diesen Brief! (lesen)

  – Hm... Dein Bruder _____ endlich fleißig? (werden)

E. Welches Verb? Complete each sentence with the correct form of **wissen** or **kennen**.

1. _____ du diese Stadt wirklich gut?

2. _____ ihr denn nicht, wo die Universität ist?

3. _____ du den Professor da?

4. Nein, ich _____ auch nicht, wie er heißt.

5. Er denkt, er _____ alles, aber wir _____ nichts.

6. Ich _____ sein Buch über Brecht. Es ist wirklich gut.

7. Du _____ doch, ich nehme jetzt Germanistik als Hauptfach.

F. An der Uni. Rewrite the following sentences, replacing the boldfaced words with the cued **der**-words.

1. **Die** Studenten machen Germanistik als Hauptfach. (manch-)

_____

2. Wir lesen jetzt **einen** Artikel über Brecht. (dies-)

_____

3. **Die** Geschichte von Brecht kennst du schon? (welch-)

_____

4. **Ein** Buch ist besonders interessant. (dies-)

_____

5. **Ein** Student muß ein Referat vorbereiten. (jed-)

_____

6. Findet ihr **den** Kurs schwer? (dies-)

_____

7. **Die** Fächer sind nicht leicht. (solch-)

_____

G. Fragen. David has questions for Nicole and her friends. Form sentences, using the cues.

1. du / mögen / Hamburg / ?

_____

2. ihr / dürfen / studieren / zehn Semester / ?

_____

3. wir / können / ansehen / die Bibliothek / jetzt / ?

_____

4. man / dürfen / aufmachen / private Unis / ?

_____

5. Studenten / müssen / schreiben / viele Klausuren / ?

_____

6. du / möchten / studieren / in Amerika / ?

_____

H. Ich möchte... Use the pictures, the vocabulary cues, and other words as appropriate to describe each situation as it really is, and the person's wish for something different. Join the factual sentence and the wish with **aber.**

vier Artikel über Brecht lesen; Bäcker werden; zwei Geschichten von Böll lesen; Kaffee trinken gehen; Metzger werden; Referat vorbereiten; schwimmen gehen; Tennis spielen

➤ sollen / möchte
  Ich *soll jetzt aufstehen, aber ich möchte eigentlich im Bett bleiben.*

1. sollen / wollen
Wir _____
_____
_____

2. sollen / möchte
Markus _____
_____
_____

3. müssen / wollen
Julia _____
_____
_____

4. müssen / wollen
Ich _____
_____
_____

I. Schönes Wochenende. Complete each sentence with the proper form of the cued verb.

1. David _____ Nicole an der Uni _____. (kennenlernen)

2. Sie (*pl.*) _____ einen Film _____. (ansehen)

3. Nicole _____ nachher _____. (müssen / einkaufen)

4. Dann _____ sie mit Karin und Max das Abendessen _____. (vorbereiten)

5. David _____ Wein _____. (mitbringen)

6. Die Vier _____ morgen die Stadt _____. (wollen / ansehen)

7. Max _____ aber immer so spät _____. (aufstehen)

J. Ich brauche Eure Notizen. Write a note to Petra and Ilse asking if they can lend you their lecture notes. Tell them you have to prepare your report, you were sick yesterday, and you still have a lot to do. Ask if they can bring the notes along tomorrow.

Liebe Petra und Ilse!

_____

_____

_____

_____

Euer / Eure

_____

K. Deutsch oder amerikanisch? Decide which system of higher education and which culture each of the following statements describes. Write **a** for **amerikanisch** or **d** for **deutsch** in each blank.

1. _____ An den Unis gibt es viele Studentenjobs.

2. _____ Es gibt zuviel Studenten.

3. _____ Es gibt viele Privatuniversitäten.

4. _____ Nach acht oder zehn Semestern macht man Examen.

5. _____ Fast° alle Studenten müssen Kurse wie Englisch | *almost*
und Mathe nehmen.

6. _____ Viele Leute gehen jeden Tag einkaufen.

7. _____ Michael kauft zwei Kilogramm Kartoffeln.

8. _____ Zum Frühstück gibt es frische Brötchen.

L. Sie haben das Wort. Respond appropriately to the following statements or questions.

Expressing Agreement

1. *Freund/in:* Kannst du mir dein Deutschbuch leihen?

   Du: _____

2. *Freund/in:* Amerikanische Studenten bekommen nur wenig oder kein Geld vom Staat.

   Du: _____

Making Excuses

3. *Freund/in:* Willst du um vier Kaffee trinken gehen?

   Du: _____

4. *Freund/in:* Kannst du mir morgen deine Notizen leihen?

   Du: _____

M. Landeskunde. Provide brief responses in English.

1. What factors determine whether a college applicant in the Federal Republic may study subjects such as law or medicine?

   _____

   _____

2. What steps has the Federal Republic taken to deal with the increased number of students desiring a university education?

   _____

   _____

N. Wo wohnen Studenten in Hamburg?   Read the passage and then answer the questions in German.

Früher° bis 1960 oder 1965 war das typische° Studentenzimmer | *formerly / typical*
eine „Studentenbude". Eine Studentenbude war ein Zimmer bei
Privatleuten. Heute wohnen nur noch sehr wenige Studenten so.
Warum ist das heute anders? Es gibt heute nicht mehr soviel alte
Häuser mit extra Zimmern. Auch möchten die Studenten endlich
machen können, was sie wollen und nicht, was der Wirt° oder die | *landlord*
Wirtin° will. Sie wollen nicht mehr hören: „Ihr Freund (oder Ihre | *landlady*
Freundin) darf aber nur bis zehn Uhr in Ihrem Zimmer bleiben."
Die Studenten wollen aber nicht nur von Wirt und Wirtin unabhängig° | *independent*
sein. Sie wollen auch von ihren Eltern unabhängig sein. Deshalb
wohnen heute auch weniger° Hamburger Studenten als früher | *fewer*
bei ihren Eltern. Die Tendenz ist, daß heute mehr Studenten ihre
eigene° Wohnung° wollen. Eine eigene Wohnung kostet° natürlich | *own / apartment / costs*
viel Geld. BAFöG bezahlt maximal aber nur DM 710 im Monat. Daher
mieten° oft mehrere° Studenten zusammen eine große Wohnung. | *rent / several*
Sie bilden° eine Wohngemeinschaft°. Weil die Wohnungen in alten | *form / group of people sharing an apartment*
Häusern oft billiger° sind als in neuen, findet man solche
Wohngemeinschaften mehr in alten und weniger° in neuen Häusern. | *cheaper | less*
Für einige Studenten hat die Universität Hamburg Studentenheime.
Studentenheime haben in der Bundesrepublik aber noch keine lange
Tradition. Es gab° eben früher Studentenbuden. Daher gibt es auch | *there were*
in Hamburg nicht genug° Plätze in Universitätsstudentenheimen. So | *enough*
kommt es, daß viele Studenten oft mehrere Monate auf° einen Platz | *for*
warten° müssen. | *wait*

1. Bis wann war das typische Studentenzimmer bei Privatleuten?

_____

2. Warum gibt es heute nicht mehr soviel Studentenbuden?

_____

3. Warum wohnen heute nicht mehr soviel Studenten bei ihren Eltern?

_____

4. Wie lange durfte früher ein Freund oder eine Freundin in einer Studentenbude bleiben?

_____

5. Warum mieten oft mehrere Studenten eine große Wohnung?

_____

6. Was ist eine Wohngemeinschaft?

_____

7. Warum mieten Studenten Wohnungen in alten Häusern?

_____

8. Warum müssen Studenten oft mehrere Monate auf einen Platz im Studentenheim warten?

_____

Kapitel 5

A. Pläne. Use the guidelines to complete the discussion between Dieter and Petra about vacation plans.

Dieter: haben / du / Pläne / für / Ferien / ?

_____

Petra: ja, / ich / fahren / nach / Dänemark

_____

Dieter: fahren / du / mit / Zug / ?

_____

Petra: nein, / ich / fliegen

_____

Dieter: wann / kommen / du / wieder / Hause / ?

_____

Petra: ich / wissen / noch nicht

_____

B. Sie haben das Wort. Respond appropriately to the following statements or questions.

Expressing Surprise

1. *Freund/in:* Ich fahre in den Ferien nach Spanien.
   Du: _____
2. *Freund/in:* Ich komme heute abend um acht nach Hause.
   Du: _____

Making Surmises

3. *Freund/in:* Warum läuft Sabine zur Uni?
   Du: _____
4. *Freund/in:* Warum fährt Markus jedes Wochenende nach Kitzbühel?
   Du: _____

C. Wieviel Kilometer? The chart gives the driving distances between pairs of German-speaking cities. Use it to answer the questions below, writing out the distances in words.

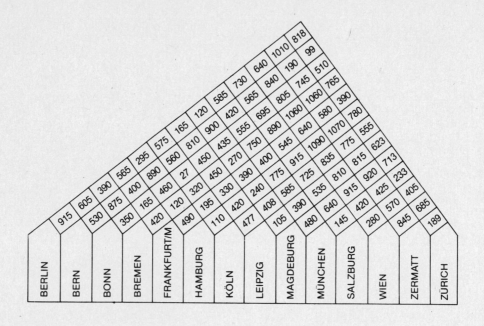

Wieviel Kilometer sind es...

1. von Wien nach Salzburg? _____

2. von Wien nach Bonn? _____

3. von Wien nach Hamburg? _____

4. von Salzburg nach München? _____

5. von Salzburg nach Bern? _____

6. von Salzburg nach Berlin? _____

D. Reisepläne. Complete the conversations in a Viennese travel agency by filling the blanks with the cued transportation terms.

1. *Student:* Kann man _____ durch die Alpen
fahren? (*by bike*)
Frau Kohl: Tja...man kann schon. Natürlich fahren die meisten Leute
_____ oder _____ .
(*by car; by train*)

2. *zwei Touristen:* Können wir _____ zur
Staatsoper° fahren? (*by streetcar*) | *state opera*

Herr Heidemann: Ja. Und es gibt auch gute Verbindungen _____
und _____ . (*by bus; by subway*)

3. *Frau Bäcker:* So, Sie wollen _____ von Frankreich
nach Amerika? (*by ship*)
Frau Seidel: Ja. Ich _____ gar nicht gern. (*fly*)

E. Identifizieren Sie! Underline each independent clause once and each dependent clause twice.

1. Do you know when you'll be going home today?

2. I'm sure that it won't be before three o'clock.

3. My car isn't running again, and it's too far to walk.

4. I'll be glad to take you, but I have to stop at the bookstore.

5. Weißt du, wohin Rita in den Ferien fährt?

6. Fährt sie nach Dänemark, oder fährt sie nach Italien?

7. Glaubst du, daß sie mit dem Zug fährt?

8. Ich kann nicht mitfahren, weil ich nicht genug Geld habe.

F. Dänemark. Complete the sentences with **aber** or **sondern,** as appropriate.

1. Ullas Großeltern kommen nicht aus Norwegen, _____ aus Dänemark.

2. Ulla kann Dänisch verstehen, _____ sie kann es nicht gut sprechen.

3. Ihre Tante wohnt noch in Dänemark, _____ ihr Onkel wohnt jetzt in Österreich.

4. In den Ferien arbeitet Ulla nicht in Innsbruck, _____ sie fährt nach Kopenhagen.

G. Kombinationen. Rewrite the sentences by combining each pair with the conjunction in parentheses. Change word order within sentences as necessary, but do not change the given order of the sentence pairs or the placement of the conjunction.

1. Ich bleibe in den Ferien zu Hause. (aber) Meine Nachbarin fährt nach Amerika.

_____

2. Ich muß im Sommer arbeiten. (weil) Ich bekomme kein Geld vom Staat.

_____

3. In den Ferien bleibt Frau Heger zu Hause. (oder) Sie fährt zu ihren Eltern.

_____

4. Wir gehen oft schwimmen. (und) Die Kinder kommen gern mit.

_____

5. Ich weiß nicht. (ob) Ich kann morgen ins Kino.

_____

6. (Weil) Ich bereite ein Referat vor. Ich muß jeden Abend arbeiten.

_____

H. Viele Fragen. Complete the answer to each of the questions, using a dependent clause.

➤ Wo arbeitet Frau Meyer jetzt?   Ich weiß nicht, *wo sie jetzt arbeitet.*

1. Wie heißt Christels Freund?

   Wir wissen nicht, _____

2. Will Christel in Linz studieren?

   Ja, ich glaube, _____

3. Ist die Uni dort groß?

   Ich weiß nicht, _____

4. Wann fährst du nach Schweden?

   Ich weiß noch nicht, _____

5. Fährt deine Freundin mit?

   Ich weiß auch nicht, _____

6. Könnt ihr zelten?

   Ja, wir glauben, _____

I. Akkusativ und Dativ. Underline each direct object once and each indirect object, when present, twice.

1. The rental agency promised us the car for next week.

2. The travel agent gave George and me several brochures.

3. Don't forget the tickets!

4. Der Deutsche fragt eine Österreicherin.

5. Diesen Dialekt kann er aber nicht verstehen.

6. Wem gibt er Geld?

7. Schenkt er seiner Freundin diese Bücher über Wien?

8. Er erzählt den Kindern eine schöne Geschichte.

J. Demonstrativpronomen. Complete the answers to the following questions, using a demonstrative pronoun.

➤ Kann man mit diesem Bus nach Oberndorf fahren?
   Ja, mit *dem* kann man nach Oberndorf fahren.

1. Kann man bei deinen Freunden in Graz schlafen?

   Ja, bei _____ kann man schlafen.

2. Können wir Erik Geld leihen?

   Ja, _____ können wir Geld leihen.

3. Wem gehören diese Bücher hier? Birgit?

   Nein, _____ gehören sie nicht.

4. Willst du deiner Schwester einen Pulli schenken?

   Ja, _____ will ich einen Pulli schenken.

5. Kann man von den Österreichern viel lernen?

   Ja, von _____ kann man viel lernen.

K. Was, wen, wem?   Answer each question, using the cues provided.

➤ Wem glaubt sie? (ihr Bruder)   *Sie glaubt ihrem Bruder.*

1. Wem dankt das Kind? (seine Eltern)

_____

2. Wen meint Erika? (der Beamte)

_____

3. Was leihst du der Studentin? (mein Heft)

_____

4. Mit wem geht Gerd in die Bibliothek? (diese Studentin)

_____

5. Wem kauft er Blumen? (seine Freunde)

_____

6. Für wen ist die Karte? (der Herr da)

_____

7. Wem gehört das Buch über Schach? (mein Onkel)

_____

8. Von wem hast du die Adresse? (das Mädchen da)

_____

9. Bei wem wohnt Peter? (eine Familie)

_____

Wo - Wer - Was - Wann?

L. Landeskunde. Provide brief responses in English.

1. Name two ways in which Austria is actively involved in world affairs.

_____

_____

2. Compare bus or train transportation in German-speaking countries with that in your own country (or city): Is it efficient? well-utilized? privately owned?

_____

_____

M. Identifizieren Sie! Identify the two rivers° and seven cities marked on the map of Austria. Refer to the map on the inside cover of your textbook as necessary. | *Flüsse*

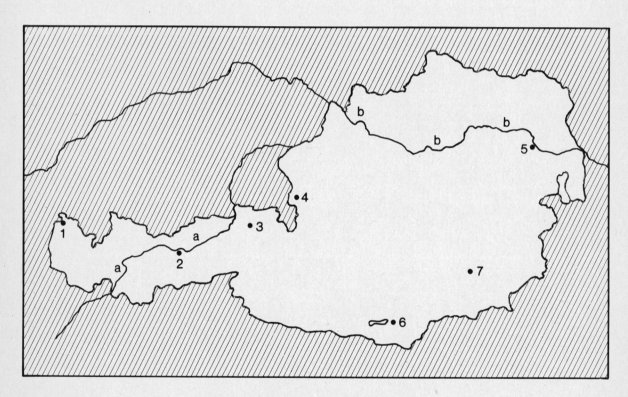

Flüsse	**Städte**	
a. _____	1. _____	5. _____
b. _____	2. _____	6. _____
	3. _____	7. _____
	4. _____	

N. Schubert und Mozart. Read the passage and then answer the questions.

Für viele Leute gehören Österreich und Musik zusammen.
Im Sommer kann man in Österreich „Musikferien" machen, denn
es gibt jeden Sommer über 50 Festspiele°, bekannte° und nicht
so bekannte, vom Bodensee im Westen bis zum Neusiedler See im
Osten. Es gibt Oper, Operette und Musical, Ballett und Konzerte
mit klassischer und moderner Musik.

    festivals / well-known

In Hohenems bei Bregenz gibt es jeden Sommer die „Schubertiade",
ein Musikfest° für die Musik von Franz Schubert (1797–1828).
Schubert ist vor allem° durch seine Lieder° bekannt. Es gibt auch
andere Musik von ihm°, zum Beispiel Symphonien, Kammermusik°
und Klavierstücke°. Aber besonders wichtig sind seine Lieder. Es
gibt über 600 von ihm.

    music festival
    vor allem: above all / songs | him (dat.) / chamber music | piano pieces | life / successful / lived | worked / piano teacher | had | own

Schubert war in seinem Leben° nicht sehr erfolgreich°. Er wohnte°
oft bei Freunden. Hier und da arbeitete° er als Klavierlehrer°. Er
hatte° immer wenig Geld. In seinem ganzen Leben hatte er kein
eigenes° Klavier.

Man erzählt von ihm diese Anekdote: Einmal will ein Freund mit
ihm ins Kaffeehaus gehen, aber Schubert kann keine Strümpfe°
ohne Löcher° finden. Er sucht und sucht und sagt endlich: „Es
scheint°, daß man in Wien die Strümpfe nur mit Löchern fabriziert."

    stockings
    holes
    seems

Die Werke° von diesem Mann findet man heute in jeder wichtigen
Bibliothek. Es sind 40 Bände°..

    works
    volumes

Die Salzburger Festspiele sind vor allem Mozartfestspiele.
Wolfgang Amadeus Mozart (1756–1791) ist in Salzburg geboren°.
Er ist für fast alle Gebiete° der° Musik sehr wichtig. Seine Opern
gehören zum internationalen Repertoire. Die großen Orchester
spielen seine Symphonien. Immer wieder° gibt es neue
Interpretationen von seinen Serenaden, von seinen Klavier–° und
Violinkonzerten° und von seinen Sonaten. Von dem großen Beethoven
(1770–1827) gibt es eine kleine Geschichte zu° Mozarts Musik:
Beethoven geht mit dem bekannten Pianisten Cramer durch einen
Park. Da spielt man Mozarts Klavierkonzert in c-Moll°. Bei einem
bestimmten Motiv bleibt Beethoven stehen°, hört eine Weile zu° und
sagt dann: „Cramer, solche Musik werde° ich in meinem Leben nicht
zustande bringen°."

    born
    areas / of
    immer wieder: again and again
    piano | Konzert: concerto
    about
    C minor / bleibt stehen: stops / hört zu: listens | will | zustande bringen: accomplish

1. Warum kann man in Österreich besonders gut Musikferien machen?

_____

2. Was für Musik gibt es bei den Festspielen?

_____

3. Welche Musik von Schubert ist besonders bekannt?

_____

4. Warum kann Schubert keine Strümpfe ohne Löcher finden?

_____

5. Wo findet man Schuberts Werke heute?

_____

6. Wo ist Mozart geboren?

_____

7. Für welche Gebiete der Musik ist Mozart wichtig? Nennen° Sie drei! | *name*

_____

8. Wie findet Beethoven Mozarts Musik?

_____

Kapitel 6

A. Wie war es? Christine tells Klaus about her dinner with Gerd. Give their conversation, based on the guidelines. Use the perfect tense where appropriate.

Christine: Tag / Klaus

_____

Klaus: Hallo / / Gerd / einladen / dich / gestern / ?

_____

Christine: Ja / wir / essen / im Ratskeller

_____

Klaus: Essen / schmecken / ?

_____

Christine: die Steaks / sein / da / phantastisch

_____

Klaus: was / ihr / trinken / ?

_____

Christine: wir / trinken / Rotwein

_____

Klaus: da / wollen / ich / essen / auch / mal

_____

B. Sie haben das Wort. Respond appropriately. See Reference Section #12 and #15 on pages R-20 and R-21 of your textbook.

Expressing Regret

1. *Freund/in:* Wir essen morgen im Ratskeller. Möchtest du mit?

   Du: _____

2. *Freund/in:* Ich habe meinen Regenmantel verloren.

   Du: _____

3. *Freund/in:* Wie gefällt dir meine Kusine?

   Du: _____

4. *Freund/in:* Nächstes Mal nehmen wir dich mit.

   Du: _____

C. Was trägt man? Complete the "clothing-tips" section of an information brochure on Mittenwald, a spa and resort in Bavaria. Use the words below in the plural, unless **ein**-words are cued.

   Anzug, Hose, Jacke, Jeans, Kleid, Pulli, Regenmantel, Sakko

   Mittenwald im Frühling! Die Tage sind schön warm, und Sie

brauchen oft nur ein_____ _____ oder ein_____

_____! Ab und zu° regnet es—daher die | *now and then*

grünen Wälder°! Bringen Sie also Ihr_____ _____ | *woods*

mit! Wenn man im Wald wandert, sind _____

immer populär. Bei Konzerten am Abend tragen Herren _____

oder _____ und Frauen _____ oder

_____ .

D. Kurze Gespräche. Use the verbs **gefallen, mögen,** and **gern haben** to complete the mini-dialogues below.

1. – Warum _____ du dieses Café nicht?

  – Ich _____ die Musik nicht _____ .

2. – _____ euch ihre Wohnung?

  – Mir _____ die sehr, aber Markus _____

  die Nachbarn nicht.

E. -*heit* und -*keit*. Write the adjective from which each noun is derived, and then guess the meaning of the noun.

	Adjective	**Meaning**
1. Künstlichkeit	_____	_____
2. Genauigkeit	_____	_____
3. Trockenheit	_____	_____
4. Gleichheit	_____	_____
5. Reinheit	_____	_____
6. Lustigkeit	_____	_____
7. Richtigkeit	_____	_____

F. Auf englisch, bitte! Write the English equivalents of the following sentences.

1. Anton meint, daß er zum Studieren zu alt ist.

_____

2. Zuviel Essen macht krank.

_____

3. Das Wandern am Morgen macht Brigitte müde.

_____

4. Warten ist oft schwer.

_____

G. Das Fußballspiel. Thomas was asked to substitute in a soccer game. Restate each sentence in the present tense.

1. Jan hat mich um elf angerufen.

_____

2. Das Spiel hat um zwei angefangen.

_____

3. Elke ist mitgekommen.

_____

4. Ich habe ziemlich schlecht gespielt.

_____

5. Einige haben das gleich bemerkt.

_____

6. Sie haben ein wenig gelächelt.

_____

7. Nach dem Spiel haben wir gefeiert.

_____

H. Geburtstagskaffee. Jürgen and Gabi are talking about Gabi's party for her father's birthday. Rewrite each sentence in the perfect tense.

1. Wir laden einige Freunde zum Kaffee ein.

_____

2. Was bekommt dein Vater zum Geburtstag?

_____

3. Das Buch gefällt meinem Vater sehr.

_____

4. Kim bäckt einen Kuchen.

_____

5. Alle probieren den Kuchen.

_____

6. Mutter erzählt den Gästen lustige Geschichten.

_____

7. Karola versteht sie nicht.

_____

8. Die Freunde bleiben bis sieben Uhr.

_____

9. Michael ißt noch ein Stück Kuchen.

_____

10. Er geht erst um zehn nach Hause.

_____

I. Abendessen. Give an account of Michael's supper with members of his study group. Rewrite, using the perfect tense in the dependent clause.

1. Michael erzählt Anna, wo er den guten Wein kauft.

_____

2. Monika versteht nicht, was er sagt.

_____

3. Sie bemerkt, daß die anderen nichts trinken.

_____

4. Peter fragt Kirstin, wo sie den guten Käse findet.

_____

5. Gerd und Steffi kommen nach dem Essen, weil sie lange arbeiten.

_____

J. Wie waren die Ferien? David tells Andreas about his trip to Austria. Give the German equivalents.

1. Why did you go by train to Austria?

_____

2. My car was broken down.

_____

3. Did you hike a lot?

_____

4. No, it rained too much.

_____

5. Did your friend like the trip?

_____

6. Not completely. Unfortunately he lost his raincoat and his money.

_____

7. Why did you stay two weeks then?

_____

K. Landeskunde. Provide brief responses in English.

1. Name three customs pertaining to restaurants in German-speaking countries which are not generally observed in your country.

_____

_____

_____

2. Name three ways in which the citizens of German-speaking countries are trying to protect the environment, and state whether such efforts are also being carried out in your community.

_____

_____

_____

L. Schreiben Sie! Write a brief conversation between Alex and Markus, in which Alex asks about the vacation Markus and his wife recently took. Use the present perfect whenever appropriate. Possible cues:

wohin / fahren?	(Bad Kissingen; in Bayern / liegen)
warum dahin?	(Ruhe / brauchen; Wälder°; Wasser)	*woods*
wie lange / bleiben?	
was / tun?	(Sport treiben: wandern, schwimmen; tanzen; essen; ins Theater gehen)
teuer?	(die Krankenkasse° / bezahlen)	*health insurance*

_____

_____

_____

_____

_____

_____

_____

_____

_____

M. Die Grünen im Hamburg. Read the passage and then answer the questions.

Seit 1982 sitzen im Hamburger Parlament (in Hamburg heißt es „Bürgerschaft°") die Grünen (genau: Grün/Alternative Liste). Wer hat sie gewählt° und warum?

Die typischen Grün-Wähler° sind jung. 73% von ihnen sind 18 bis 35. Besonders oft wählen° Studenten Grün. Außerdem wählen besonders viele Leute da Grün, wo die Luft und das Wasser stinken oder das Land kaputt ist. Ein Problem ist zum Beispiel die Elbe. Die Elbe ist die Wasserstraße von Hamburg zur Nordsee. Für die großen Schiffe muß sie tief° sein. Man hat sie also tief gemacht. Den Sand aus der Elbe hat man aufs° Land gepumpt. Im Elbsand sind aber Metalle wie Cadmium, und die hat man dann bald im Trinkwasser gefunden. Das Problem in Hamburg ist nicht zuwenig Wasser, es ist zuwenig sauberes° Wasser, sagen die Grünen.

Ein anderes Problem ist die Luft. In einigen Stadtteilen stinkt sie nach Gas, und es gibt zuviel Staub° in der Luft. Bis jetzt hat die Industrie ihre Verschmutzung° selbst gemessen°. Die Grünen sagen, daß von 7000 bis 8000 Firmen aber nur 144 es wirklich getan haben. Die Grünen finden nicht, daß das genug ist. Viele Wähler auch nicht. Deshalb haben die alten Parteien, vor allem die Sozialdemokraten (SPD), Wähler verloren. Diese Wähler haben die neue Partei, die Grünen, gewählt. Die Grünen sitzen nun im Parlament in der Opposition und machen den alten Parteien das Leben schwer.

citizens' council
elected
voters
vote

deep
on the

clean

dust
pollution / measured

1. Welche neue Partei sitzt erst wenige Jahre im Hamburger Parlament?

_____

2. Wie alt sind die typischen Grün-Wähler?

_____

3. Warum muß die Elbe tief sein?

_____

4. Was ist mit dem Elbsand los?

_____

5. Was ist das Trinkwasserproblem in Hamburg?

_____

6. Was ist in einigen Stadtteilen mit der Luft los?

_____

7. Wer hat Wähler verloren?

_____

8. Wo im Parlament sitzen die Grünen?

_____

UMWELT SCHUTZ
geht jeden an

• • • • • • • • • • • • • • • • • • •

Salzstreuung schädigt unsere Grün-
flächen und führt zur Bodenversalzung!

Streusalz soll daher, auch im privaten
Bereich, weitestgehend durch umwelt-
freundliche, mechanisch wirksame Streu-
mittel (Splitt, Sand, ...) ersetzt
werden.

Das Landratsamt
informiert Sie gerne
Tel.: 07461/96 368

Altglas ist Rohstoff

Kapitel 7

A. Eine Einladung. Bärbel tries to convince Axel to go for a drink after the seminar. Give the German equivalent of their conversation.

Axel: What are you doing after the lecture?

_____

Bärbel: I'm meeting Karin at the *Ratskeller;* would you like to come along?

_____

Axel: No thanks, it's much too loud there.

_____

Bärbel: How about a beer garden? There we can sit outside.

_____

Axel: Fine, but I'm broke.

_____

Bärbel: It doesn't matter. I'll treat.

_____

Axel: Great, I'll see you then at the beer garden.

_____

B. Was meinen Sie? Decide whether each sentence is a subjective judgment or generalization or an objective observation. Write **U** for **Urteil°** or **B** for **Beobachtung°**. | *judgment / observation*

1. _____ Die Amerikaner sehen den ganzen Tag fern.

2. _____ Die Deutschen geben die Hand, wenn sie „Guten Tag" sagen.

3. _____ Die Amerikaner benutzen den Vornamen mehr als die Deutschen.

4. _____ Die Deutschen fahren wie die Wilden.

5. _____ Die Amerikaner gehen nicht oft zu Fuß.

6. _____ Die deutschen Züge sind fast immer pünktlich.

7. _____ Man findet Parks in vielen deutschen Städten.

8. _____ In deutschen Restaurants stehen Blumen auf den Tischen.

9. _____ Die Deutschen essen zuviel Wurst.

10. _____ Die Amerikaner essen zu schnell.

11. _____ Die Geschäfte in der Bundesrepublik sind abends geschlossen.

12. _____ Die Amerikaner sind sehr freundlich.

C. Sie haben das Wort. Respond appropriately. See Reference Section #1 and #17 on pages R-19 and R-21 of your textbook.

Expressing Skepticism

1. *Freund/in:* Die amerikanische Bürokratie ist nicht so schlimm wie die deutsche.

   Du: _____

2. *Freund/in:* Kuchen mit künstlichen Farben schmeckt furchtbar.

   Du: _____

Expressing Joy and Pleasure

3. *Freund/in:* Möchtest du morgen bei mir fernsehen?

   Du: _____

4. *Freund/in:* Am Samstag gehen wir ins Café Krone.

   Du: _____

D. Bei Axel. Axel's friends are meeting at his house before going to a party. Describe their positions in the room and what they are doing by completing each sentence with an appropriate preposition. Contract the definite articles in parentheses.

1. Paul steht _____ Claudia.

2. Sie sprechen _____ das Wetter.

3. Drei Freunde sitzen _____ (dem) Tisch.

4. Uwe schreibt eine Karte _____ seine Freundin.

5. Hans redet _____ seine Ferien.

6. Wer sitzt _____ Hans und Uwe?

7. Gisela kommt _____ (das) Zimmer.

8. Paul und Claudia stehen _____ dem Sofa.

E. Akkusativ oder Dativ?   Write six sentences, using a different either-or preposition in each sentence. For the first three sentences, pick an object from the list below and describe its location at this moment. Make sure the object is appropriate for the cued verb.

➤ (liegen) Heft   *Mein Heft liegt jetzt auf meinem Tisch.*

For the last three sentences, pick three more objects from the list and describe where you put each one earlier. Again, make sure the object is appropriate for the cued verb.

➤ (legen) Bleistift   *Ich habe meinen Bleistift neben mein Buch gelegt.*

Auto, Bild, Blumen, Deutschbuch, Geld, Glas, Kuli, Mantel, Rad, Schuhe, Tasche, Uhr

1. (stehen) _____

2. (liegen) _____

3. (hängen) _____

4. (legen) _____

5. (stecken) _____

6. (stellen) _____

F. Welche Präpositionen?   Complete each sentence with a preposition, a definite article or possessive adjective, and the noun in parentheses. Contract the definite article with the preposition whenever possible.

➤ Am Montag geht Frau Gerber _____. (Markt)
Am Montag geht Frau Gerber auf den Markt.

1. Sitzt Rolf noch _____? (Tisch)

2. Jürgen geht _____. (Universität Heidelberg)

3. Diane denkt oft _____. (Ferien in Italien)

4. Wie schnell fährst du _____? (Autobahn)

5. Marianne hält viel _____. (Professor)

6. Andrea studiert jetzt _____. (Universität)

7. Maria arbeitet wieder _____. (Supermarkt)

8. Gehst du morgen _____? (Stadt)

G. Fragen, Fragen! Oldenburg's information center receives many inquiries about events in the city. Complete the answers below with the appropriate accusative and dative time expressions.

1. – Wie lange spielt „Figaros Hochzeit°"? | *Marriage of Figaro*

    – Sie spielt _____ . (*one month*)

2. – Wann ist der erste Winterflohmarkt°? | *winter flea market*

    – Er ist _____ . (*on Saturday*)

3. – Wann ist das Weihnachtskonzert im Schloß°? | *castle*

    – Es tut mir leid, das war schon _____ .

      (*a week ago*)

4. – Kommt das Hazen-Quartett wieder?

    – Ja, es kommt bestimmt _____ wieder.

      (*next year*)

5. – Wann kann man Karten fürs Staatstheater kaufen?

    – Man kann sie _____ ab 14. Uhr kaufen. (*every day*)

H. Pronomen. Complete each pair of sentences with a pronoun that corresponds to the pronoun in boldface.

1. Was macht ihr heute abend? Ich möchte _____ einladen.

2. Du weißt nicht, wer **sie** ist? Du kennst _____ also nicht.

3. **Wir** fahren oft in die Schweiz, weil _____ das Land gefällt.

4. Warum essen **Sie** den Kuchen nicht? Schmeckt er _____ nicht?

5. **Ich** schenke ihr die Blumen. Sie dankt _____ dafür.

6. **Er** weiß alles. Fragen Sie _____ !

7. Ich sehe, daß **du** müde bist. Ich kenne _____ gut.

8. **Sie** hat ihren Bleistift verloren. Leih _____ doch deinen Bleistift!

I. Schenkt er es ihnen? Your friend Thomas wants to know whether you're giving away the items mentioned. Tell him he is right, using object pronouns.

➥ Schenkst du Karin diese Bluse?   *Ja, ich schenke sie ihr.*

1. Kaufst du deinen Eltern dieses Radio? _____

2. Schenkst du deiner Mutter diese Handschuhe? _____

3. Kaufst du deinem Bruder diesen Pulli? _____

4. Schenkst du dem Nachbarskind dieses Buch? _____

5. Kaufst du mir diese Schokolade? _____

6. Schenkst du uns diese Karten? _____

J. Variationen. First rewrite, using a subject pronoun and replacing the words in boldface with a **da**-compound or a preposition with a pronoun. Then rewrite as a specific question, using a **wo**-compound or a preposition with a pronoun.

➤ Jan spricht gern **über den Film.**   *Er spricht gern darüber.*
                                          Worüber spricht er gern?

1. Helmut arbeitet schon lange **an seinem Buch.**

_____

_____

2. Frau und Herr Becker spielen gern **mit ihren Kindern.**

_____

_____

3. Scherers sprechen oft **von ihrer Reise.**

_____

_____

4. Karl kocht viel **für seine Freundin.**

_____

_____

5. Nadine schreibt nur **mit ihrem neuen Kugelschreiber.**

_____

_____

K. Typisch amerikanisch? Read the passage and then answer the questions.

Ein „typischer" Amerikaner sagt: „Also, wissen Sie, ich bin
ja ganz gern in der Bundesrepublik gewesen. Aber ich möchte
in diesem Land nicht leben. Ich fahre zum Beispiel gern mit dem
Auto. Aber das Land ist zu klein. In *einem* Tag bin ich von Hamburg
im Norden nach München im Süden gefahren. Nicht ganz 800 Kilometer.
Nördlich von Hamburg ist dann nicht mehr viel, südlich von München
auch nicht. Ich weiß, die Deutschen wandern gern, oder sie gehen
spazieren°, in den Parks, an den Seen° und auch in den Stadtzentren°. | *go for a walk /*
Wirklich! Aber ich arbeite die ganze Woche. Also will ich am Wochenende | *lakes / city centers*
doch nicht auch noch wandern. Man sieht auch nicht soviel, wenn man zu
Fuß geht.
„Und dann die Restaurants! Das Essen war ja nicht schlecht. Darüber will
ich ja nichts sagen. Aber nie steht kaltes Wasser auf dem Tisch. Und wenn
die Kellner° kaltes Wasser bringen, ist es ein Miniglas, und darin schwimmt | *waiters*

dann ein klitzekleines° Eisstück°. Ich will schließlich trinken und keine | *tiny / ice cube*
Pillen nehmen. Das deutsche Bier habe ich aber zu schwer und zu bitter und
zu warm gefunden. Und der deutsche Wein war mir zu sauer.

  „Und dann habe ich immer ,Herr Schmidt' gesagt und ,Frau Meyer'.
Wie kalt das ist. Und zu mir haben alle Leute ,Herr Jones' gesagt. Ich
habe das furchtbar unpersönlich gefunden. Daher habe ich auch keine
Freunde in diesem Land, obwohl° ich doch drei Wochen da war. Wenn | *although*
Sie mich fragen, ob ich eines Tages wieder dahin will, so muß ich sagen,
eigentlich nicht."

1. Wo möchte Herr Jones nicht leben?

_____

2. Warum kann er in diesem Land nicht so gut mit dem Auto fahren?

_____

3. Warum will er am Wochenende nicht wandern?

_____

4. Was gefällt ihm nicht, wenn er zu Fuß geht?

_____

5. Was hat ihm in den Restaurants geschmeckt?

_____

6. Was hat ihm nicht gefallen?

_____

7. Warum hat ihm das Bier nicht geschmeckt?

_____

8. Wie findet er es, wenn er Herr und Frau benutzen muß und wenn die Leute zu ihm „Herr
   Jones" sagen?

_____

9. Warum hat er keine Freunde in der Bundesrepublik?

_____

L. Landeskunde. Provide brief responses in English.

1. Compare two ways in which television in the Federal Republic of Germany differs from television in your own country.

_____

_____

2. With whom do German-speaking people use the word **Freund?** Name two or three adjectives that English speakers often use with the noun *friend*.

_____

_____

M. Schreiben Sie! Answer the following questions and give a brief explanation.

1. An wen denken Sie oft? Warum?

_____

_____

2. Wovor haben Sie Angst? Warum?

_____

_____

3. Wovor haben Sie keine Angst? Warum nicht?

_____

_____

4. Mit wem reden Sie gern? Warum?

_____

_____

5. Wohin gehen Sie gern mit Freunden? Warum?

_____

_____

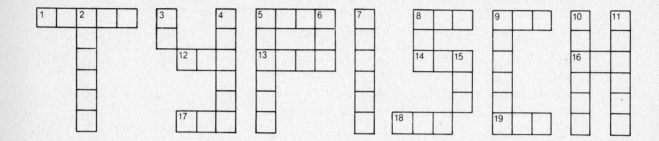

Waagerecht (horizontal)

1. fear
5. tree
8. her (*dat.*)
9. them (*acc.*)
12. on; at; to
13. loud
14. me (*dat.*)
16. be (*fam. sg.*), as in *Be quiet!*
17. once (*abbr.*), as in *We saw him once in Berlin.*
18. narrow
19. red

Senkrecht (vertical)

2. forks
3. on; at; to
4. feeling
5. pictures
6. with
7. pub
8. him (*dat.*)
9. clean
10. knives
11. pages
15. bike

Kapitel 8

A. Die Fete. Read the following conversation and then make up five questions about it. Answer your own questions.

Susanne: 0 je, hier sieht es aber furchtbar aus.
Ingrid: Und in einer Stunde kommen schon die Gäste.
Susanne: Wieviel Leute kommen eigentlich?
Ingrid: Ich habe fünfzehn Leute eingeladen.
Susanne: Ich räume schnell auf.
Ingrid: Hoffentlich bringt Jan seine neuen Kassetten mit.
Susanne: Hast du jetzt einen neuen Kassettenrecorder?
Ingrid: Ja, sieh mal, das Geburtstagsgeschenk meiner Eltern!
Susanne: Na, dann muß die Fete ja toll werden.

1. _____

_____

2. _____

_____

3. _____

_____

4. _____

_____

5. _____

_____

B. Sie haben das Wort. Respond appropriately. See Reference Section #6 and #3 on pages R-20 and R-19 of your textbook.

Expressing Good Wishes

1. *Freund/in:* Ich habe gestern Geburtstag gehabt.

Du: _____

2. *Freund/in:* Morgen fahre ich mit Anne und Erik in die Berge.

Du: _____

Expressing Annoyance

3. **Freund/in:** Ich habe dreißig Leute für heute abend eingeladen.

   Du: _____

4. **Freund/in:** Ich habe Max deine Stereoanlage geliehen.

   Du: _____

C. Ferienreise. Complete the information about the Kohls' trip to Austria by providing the proper genitive forms of the noun phrases in parentheses.

1. Sie hatten die Adresse _____ in Salzburg. (ein Freund)

2. Auf einer Fete haben Kohls den Nachbarn _____ kennengelernt. (ihre Freunde)

3. Sie haben den Sohn _____ auch kennengelernt. (der Nachbar)

4. Während _____ mußte Frau Kohl manchmal arbeiten. (die Abendstunden)

5. Wegen _____ war sie oft müde. (ihre Arbeit)

6. Wegen _____ sind Kohls nicht viel gewandert. (das Wetter)

7. Kohls konnten nur fünf Tage statt _____ in Österreich bleiben. (eine Woche)

8. Trotz _____ haben die Ferien der Familie gefallen. (die Schwierig-keiten)

D. Wie bitte? Mrs. Fischer is telling her husband about a new employee. Mr. Fischer is distracted and asks a question about each statement. Write his questions, beginning each one with an appropriate question word from the following list:

wann, was, wen, wessen, wie, wie alt, wo, woher, wohin

➤ Der junge Mann heißt Markus Goebler.   *Wie heißt der junge Mann?*

1. Markus ist 25 Jahre alt. _____

2. Er kommt aus Bonn. _____

3. Er hat in München studiert. _____

4. Er hat Psychologie studiert. _____

5. Markus fliegt nach Amerika. _____

6. Er kommt am achten Februar an. _____

7. Er besucht seine Freundin Katrin. _____

8. Katrins Familie kommt aus Graz. _____

E. Akjektivendungen. Fill in each blank with the proper adjective ending. If no ending is required, enter an X.

1. Gestern habe ich einen interessant_____ Film gesehen.

2. Die Filmschauspieler° waren aber nicht sehr bekannt_____. | *actors*

3. Hinter dem Kino steht ein alt_____ Café.

4. Trotz des offen_____ Fensters war es warm im Café.

5. Ich mag natürlich_____ Lebensmittel gern, aber David hat

   der Kuchen mit den rot_____ und grün_____ Farben gut

   geschmeckt.

6. Heute sind wir ins neu_____ Kaufhaus gegangen.

7. Im dritt_____ Stock findet man Möbel°. | *furniture*

8. Ich brauche eine neu_____ Lampe und einen neu_____ Stuhl.

9. Ein schwarz_____ Stuhl war besonders schön_____,

   aber zu teuer_____ .

10. In dem klein_____Restaurant neben dem Kaufhaus gibt es immer

    gut_____ Essen.

F. Was meinen Sie? State your opinion by choosing one or more of the adjectives in parentheses, or provide your own.

1. Ich möchte ein _____ Auto haben. (klein, groß, billig, teuer)

2. Ich gehe gern zu _____ Feten. (lustig, klein, laut, interessant)

3. Ich möchte einen _____ Pulli kaufen. (warm, rot, leicht, toll)

4. Ich sehe gern _____ Filme. (schön, modern, alt, gut, lustig)

5. Herr X ist ein _____ Professor. (gut, intelligent, doof, ausgezeich-

   net, nett)

G. Alles im Singular. Rewrite each sentence, changing all nouns (and the verb if necessary) to the singular.

1. Die Gärten der neuen Häuser sind zu klein.

_____

2. Die Türen der österreichischen Wohnungen sind immer geschlossen.

_____

3. Haben Sie die Namen der amerikanischen Gäste verstanden?

_____

4. Möchtest du meine neuen Kassetten hören?

_____

5. Die alten Lieder gefallen mir sehr.

_____

6. Man kann die Menschen auf der österreichischen Terrassen nicht leicht sehen.

_____

7. Die Referate der deutschen Studenten waren nicht gut.

_____

H. Zu laut. Karen is telling about Barbara's experiences in Vienna. The room is noisy and you're having trouble hearing. Ask to have several statements repeated by forming questions using **was für (ein)** or **welch**. **Was für (ein)** asks a general question requiring a description or an explanation. **Welch** asks a question about a specific group of persons or things. The answer contains a definite article or a possessive pronoun.

➤ Sie wohnt in einer *ruhigen* Straße.   *In was für einer Straße wohnt sie?*

➤ Sie besucht heute ihre *Literatur*vorlesung.   *Welche Vorlesung besucht sie heute?*

1. Barbara studiert an der Universität *Wien*.

_____

2. Die *Universitäts*bibliothek ist ausgezeichnet.

_____

3. Barbara wohnt bei einer *netten* Familie.

_____

4. Die Familie wohnt in einem *schönen alten* Haus.

_____

5. Ihre *Zimmer*tür ist immer offen.

_____

6. *Offene* Türen stören die Österreicher.

_____

I. Wie sieht es aus?   Describe five rooms of your house or apartment.

➡ *Ich habe eine moderne, schöne Küche.*

_____

_____

_____

_____

J. Landeskunde.   Provide brief responses in English.

1. Compare opportunities or places to shop in German-speaking cities with those in your country.

_____

_____

2. Name three features of homes in German-speaking countries (home design and/or appointments) that promote a sense of privacy.

_____

_____

K. Automatisch.   Read the passage and then answer the questions.

Viele Österreicher schließen die Türen ihrer Zimmer und ihrer Büros mehr oder weniger° automatisch. Man kann zeigen, daß sie viele Sachen automatisch tun und sagen und auch denken und erwarten°. Wenn sie „Guten Tag" sagen, geben sie einander fast automatisch die Hand. Wenn sie an das Wort „Bekannte" denken, dann denken sie auch an Nachnamen° und „Sie". Sie haben viele Bekannte, aber nur wenige Freunde, und zu den wenigen Freunden sagen sie natürlich „du".

Wenn ein Bekannter sagt: „Ich treff' Sie im Café", dann weiß man automatisch, was man von einem Café erwarten kann. Man weiß, daß viele Österreicher vor allem am Nachmittag ins Café gehen, daß sie dort meistens Kaffee trinken und Kuchen essen, daß viele wegen der netten Atmosphäre hingehen, daß oft Blumen auf den kleinen Tischen stehen, daß man dort bei einem Kaffee den ganzen Nachmittag sitzen kann.

Oder ein Vater sagt zum Beispiel zu seinem Freund: „Unsere Tochter ist jetzt auch Studentin." Da weiß der Freund, daß sie auf eine Universität geht. Er fragt vielleicht: „Was will deine Tochter denn werden? Apothekerin, Lehrerin°, Ärztin?" Oder: „Im wievielten Semester ist sie, noch im ersten oder schon im zweiten?" Oder: „Nach wieviel Semestern kann sie in ihrem Fach denn Examen machen?"

mehr...weniger: more or less

expect

surnames

teacher

1. Welche Türen schließen viele Österreicher automatisch?

_____

2. Was tun sie automatisch, wenn sie „Guten Tag" sagen?

_____

3. Haben die Österreicher mehr Freunde oder mehr Bekannte?

_____

4. Was sagen die Österreicher zu ihren Freunden?

_____

5. Warum gehen viele Österreicher ins Café?

_____

6. Was steht in einem netten Café meistens auf dem Tisch?

_____

7. Wie oft muß man etwas bestellen, wenn man den ganzen Nachmittag im Café sitzen will?

_____

8. Im wievielten Semester ist man, wenn man gerade angefangen hat zu studieren?

_____

L. Liebes Tagebuch°. Keep a diary for three days. Follow the | _diary_
model below for the dates, and use the perfect tense in your entries.

➤ _Freitag, den zwölften Februar: Heute habe ich Barbara im Café getroffen. Am Abend bin ich mit ihr ins Kino gegangen._

_____, den _____ _____: _____

_____

_____

_____, den _____ _____: _____

_____

_____

_____, den _____ _____: _____

_____

_____

Kapitel 9

A. Ein Gespräch. Use the background information below to write a conversation between Michael and Klaus.

Gestern war Michael mit seinen Freunden bei einem Picknick. Leider war es kalt, und dann hat es auch noch geregnet. Heute hat er Fieber. Er hat noch viel zu arbeiten für die Klausur und keine Zeit, zum Arzt zu gehen. Klaus besucht ihn.

_____

_____

_____

_____

_____

_____

B. Sie haben das Wort. Respond appropriately. See Reference Sections #12 and #14 on pages R-20 and R-21 of your textbook.

Expressing Regret

1. *Freund/in:* Jan tut das Bein sehr weh.
   Du: _____

2. *Freund/in:* Ich bin furchtbar erkältet. Ich kann nicht mit zum Ski laufen.
   Du: _____

Expressing Indifference

3. *Freund/in:* Möchtest du morgen Ski laufen?
   Du: _____

4. *Freund/in:* Sollen wir mit dem Auto oder mit dem Rad fahren?
   Du: _____

C. Einkaufen. Nicole and Daniel are shopping for birthday presents for Karin. Give the English equivalent of each sentence in boldface.

1. **In diesem Geschäft gibt es viel Interessantes zu sehen.**

_____

2. **Es ist aber nicht leicht, etwas Schönes und Billiges zu finden.**

_____

3. **Die kleinen Sachen sind oft die schönsten.**

_____

4. **Karin liest gern, nicht? —Ja, aber sie hört lieber Musik.**

_____

5. **Du verstehst mehr von Musik als ich. Was hältst du von diesen Kassetten?**

_____

6. **Sie sind toll und nicht so teuer wie die anderen.**

_____

7. **Schenkst du Karin das kleine Poster? —Nein, das größere.**

_____

8. **Es ist moderner.**

_____

D. Komparativ und Superlativ. Rewrite each sentence twice, first with the comparative of the adjective or adverb, and then with the superlative.

➤ Das Zimmer ist schön.   Die Wohnung _ist schöner._
                                           Das Haus _ist am schönsten._

1. Basel gefällt mir gut.

   Zürich _____

   Luzern _____

2. Müllers reisen viel.

   Herr Gerber _____

   Frau Böhm _____

3. Die Preise° bei Becker sind hoch. | _prices_

   Die Preise bei Schmitt _____

   Die Preise bei Klein _____

4. Ich rede gern über Sport.

   Ich _____ über Musik.

   Ich _____ über Schach.

SCHÖNER
SEHEN

OPTIK AM KLEISTPARK
Hauptstraße 158
1000 Berlin 62
☎030 - 781 32 60

E. In welchem Land? Answer the following questions about the **Lebensstandardtabelle°**.

standard of living table

LEBENSSTANDARDTABELLE

T - Tage
S - Stunden
M - Minuten

	USA			Bundesrepublik Deutschland			DDR			SCHWEIZ		
	T	S	M	T	S	M	T	S	M	T	S	M
Brot, 1 kg			10			11			9			6
Bier, 1 l			7			8			33			8
Farbfernseher (59 cm)	9	2	4	15	2	42	122	3	3	17	2	40
Fahrrad	1	7	54	4	6	38	6	6	23	2	5	20
Auto	155	5	55	173	2	18	660	4	26	196	6	40
Kühlschrank	12	7	33	10	1	45	74	0	36	8	5	30

1. Wer muß länger für ein Kilo Brot arbeiten, die Arbeiter der Bundesrepublik oder die Arbeiter der Schweiz?

_____

2. Wer muß am wenigsten für einen Kühlschrank arbeiten?

_____

3. Wo ist ein Fahrrad für die Arbeiter billiger, in der Schweiz oder in der Bundesrepublik?

_____

4. Wo kostet ein Auto für die Arbeiter am wenigsten, in den USA, in der DDR oder in der Schweiz?

_____

5. In welchem Land ist Bier am billigsten?

_____

6. Wer muß weniger für einen Farbfernseher arbeiten, die Arbeiter in der Bundesrepublik oder die Arbeiter in der Schweiz?

_____

F. Reflexivpronomen. In the brief conversations below, complete each sentence with the appropriate reflexive pronoun.

1. Hat Inge _____ schon die Zähne geputzt?

   Ja, aber Julia hat _____ noch nicht geduscht.

2. Willst du _____ einen neuen Pulli kaufen?

   Ja, wir können gleich gehen. Ich ziehe _____ schnell eine Jacke an.

3. Hast du _____ erkältet?

   Leider, ich fühle _____ nicht wohl.

4. Wir fragen _____, warum Anja nicht gekommen ist.

   Wir können es _____ auch nicht erklären.

5. Herr Kleiner, setzen Sie _____ bitte!

   Ich habe _____ schon ein Glas Wein bestellt. Was darf ich für Sie bestellen?

G. Auf der Uni. Tell about Tanja's first semester. Write new sentences using the modal + infinitive, zu + infinitive, or **um...zu** + infinitive constructions, as appropriate. Begin each sentence with the phrase in parentheses.

➤ Tanja lernt Japanisch. (Es ist schwer,...)
   Es ist schwer, Japanisch zu lernen.

1. Sie versteht alles. (Sie versucht,...)

   _____

2. Tanjas Freunde reden oft über ihre Kurse. (Tanjas Freunde wollen...)

   _____

3. Tanja schreibt ein Referat. (Tanja muß...)

   _____

4. Sie sieht nicht fern. (Sie hat keine Zeit...)

   _____

5. Sie kommt schneller zur Uni. (Sie hat sich ein Rad gekauft,...)

   _____

6. Sie kauft nicht jeden Tag ein. (Sie braucht nicht...)

   _____

H. Identifizieren Sie! Identify the two rivers (**Flüsse**) and eight cities marked on the map of Switzerland. Refer to the map on the inside cover of your textbook as necessary.

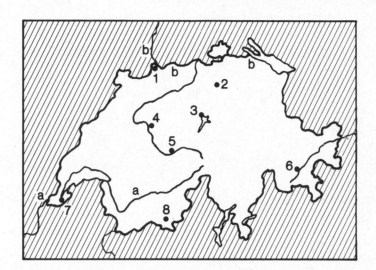

Flüsse

a. _____

b. _____

Städte

1. _____

2. _____

3. _____

4. _____

5. _____

6. _____

7. _____

8. _____

I. Alternative Energie. Read the passage and then answer the questions.

Michael Mahler ist Mechaniker°. Seine Frau Marianne ist Studentin.   *mechanic*
Sie wohnen in Zürich und leben mit alternativer Energie. Und das
ist so gekommen: Das Elektrizitätswerk° hat, so glauben sie, mit dem   *power company*
Geld der Kunden° ein Atomkraftwerk° finanziert. Um zu zeigen, daß sie   *customers / nu-*
dagegen waren, haben sie jeden Monat nur 90 Prozent ihrer Rechnung°   *clear power plant*
bezahlt. Sie waren dagegen, als Kunden des Elektrizitätswerks ein   *bill*
Atomkraftwerk zu finanzieren. Nach einiger Zeit hat ihnen das
Elektrizitätswerk die Elektrizität abgestellt°.   *turned off*

Nun machen sie ihre eigene mit einem Fahrrad auf einem Stand
im Wohnzimmer. Ein Dynamo° produziert 100 bis 150 Watt. Die gehen   *generator*
in fünf Autobatterien auf einem Bücherregal. Am Fenster haben sie noch
einen Generator. Der arbeitet mit Solarenergie. Jeden Tag müssen sie eine
halbe Stunde „radfahren", um ihre tägliche Elektrizität zu produzieren.

Natürlich sind sie jetzt viel vorsichtiger° mit der Elektrizität. Ihren | *more careful*
Fernseher haben sie verkauft. Die meisten Programme waren sowieso° | *anyhow*
nicht sehr gut. Einen Kühlschrank brauchen sie auch nicht, denn sie
essen vor allem frisches Obst und Gemüse. Sie benutzen noch elektrisches
Licht und einen Staubsauger°. Ihre Stereoanlage spielen sie viel weniger | *vacuum cleaner*
als früher. Sie haben sich ein besseres Radio mit Batterie gekauft. Sie
finden es nicht mehr so furchtbar, sich kalt zu duschen. Wenn sie heiß
baden wollen, stellen sie die Badewanne ins Wohnzimmer und machen
Wasser auf dem Herd° heiß. Am schwierigsten ist es mit der | *stove*
Waschmaschine, weil das Wasser meistens nicht richtig warm wird.

Auf die Frage, ob das ein Modell für andere ist, antworten die Zwei:
„Es ist keine Frage, daß unsere Elektrizitätsproduktion umweltfreundlicher
ist. Die Frage ist eben, was man wichtiger findet, persönlichen Komfort
oder Umwelt. Auf diese Frage muß jeder für sich selbst eine Antwort geben.“

1. Mit was für Energie leben Michael und Marianne?

_____

2. Warum haben sie nur 90 Prozent ihrer Rechnungen bezahlt?

_____

3. Warum machen sie ihre eigene Energie?

_____

4. Wie produzieren sie Energie?

_____

5. Warum haben sie ihren Fernseher verkauft?

_____

6. Warum brauchen sie keinen Kühlschrank?

_____

7. Was benutzen sie oft anstatt ihrer Stereoanlage?

_____

8. Wie duschen sie sich?

_____

9. Wer produziert umweltfreundlichere Energie, Michael und Marianne oder das
   Elektrizitätswerk?

_____

J. Landeskunde. Provide brief responses in English.

1. Compare how one becomes a naturalized citizen in Switzerland and in your country.

_____

_____

2. Name one major political similarity and one major political difference between Switzerland and your country.

_____

_____

K. Schreiben Sie! Compare yourself with a friend or relative in terms of appearance and likes and dislikes. You may use all or some of the questions below:

1. Was lesen Sie und sie/er?
2. Was machen Sie in Ihrer und sie/er in ihrer/seiner Freizeit?
3. Was für Sachen tragen Sie und sie/er?
4. Was möchten Sie und sie/er werden?
5. Wie sehen Sie und sie/er aus?

_____

_____

_____

_____

_____

_____

Verkehrsverein Bern
CH-3001 Bern/Switzerland

Schweiz
Suisse
Svizzera
Switzerland

L. Extra-Übung: Kreuzworträtsel°. Complete the following puzzle. | *crossword puzzle*

Waagerecht

1. to begin
4. air
7. foot
8. face
11. short
12. acquaintance
13. how much
14. kitchen
16. be!
17. come!
18. (I) look at (*dependent clause*)
20. (he) makes

Senkrecht

1. on
2. excellent
3. several
5. free
6. (I) sleep
9. (I) do
10. advertisements
14. (you, *fam. pl.*) can
15. (I) eat
17. cook!
19. since, because

Kapitel 10

A. Eine neue Stelle. Assume you are interviewing for a job as a programmer. Answer the following questions according to your personal preference.

Personalchef/in: Warum sind Sie Programmierer/in geworden?

Sie: _____

_____

Personalchef/in: Haben Sie schon einmal in einer Firma gearbeitet? Bei welcher?

Sie: _____

_____

Personalchef/in: Welche Fremdsprachen sprechen Sie?

Sie: _____

_____

Personalchef/in: Wieviel Computersprachen können Sie? Welche?

Sie: _____

_____

Personalchef/in: Reisen Sie gern?

Sie: _____

_____

Personalchef/in: Was möchten Sie gern verdienen?

Sie: _____

_____

B. Sie haben das Wort. Respond appropriately. See Reference Sections #2 and #9 on pages R-19 and R-20 of your textbook.

Expressing Doubt

1. *Freund/in:* Bei einer größeren Firma bekomme ich mehr Verantwortung.
   Du: _____

2. *Freund/in:* Deine Chefin kann fließend Spanisch, nicht?
   Du: _____

Expressing Surprise

3. *Freund/in:* Ich wollte eigentlich Zahnarzt/Zahnärztin werden.
   Du: _____

4. *Freund/in:* Sebastian hat seine Stelle schon wieder gewechselt.
   Du: _____

C. Bewerbung° bei Lufthansa. Complete the following sections of a job application form for Lufthansa German Airlines.

| *job application*

Persönliche Daten zur Bewerbung als Flugbegleiter°

Raum für Lichtbild

(bitte einkleben, wenn Sie mit dem Verbleib eines Fotos bei LH einverstanden sind)

Name:

Vorname:

Geburtsdatum:

Geburtsort: Staatsangehörigkeit:[2]

derzeitiger[3] Wohnort ☐   Straße:

                                                 Stadt:

                                                 Telefon:

Sprachkenntnisse[4] Deutsch   ☐ fließend   ☐ gut   ☐ teilweise[5]

Fremdsprachenkenntnisse

Englisch-Konversation   ☐ fließend   ☐ gut   ☐ teilweise

Französisch-Konversation   ☐ fließend   ☐ gut   ☐ teilweise

Spanisch-Konversation   ☐ fließend   ☐ gut   ☐ teilweise

andere Sprachen   ☐ fließend   ☐ gut   ☐ teilweise

welche Hobbies haben Sie?

haben Sie sich schon einmal bei der Deutschen Lufthansa beworben?[6]   ☐ ja   ☐ nein

der Grund für die jetzige Bewerbung ist:[7]

[1] *flight attendant*   [2] *citizenship*   [3] *current*   [4] *linguistic knowledge*   [5] *some*   [6] *applied*   [7] *reason*

D. Ein neues Leben. Describe what occurs when Mrs. Gerber returns to work. Rewrite each sentence in the present tense.

1. Der Vater mußte lernen, wie man kocht.

_____

2. Klaus wusch jeden Tag ab.

_____

3. Seine Schwester trocknete immer ab.

_____

4. Alle lernten zu helfen.

_____

5. Die Nachbarn hatten Vorurteile.

_____

6. Sie kritisierten Frau Gerber.

_____

7. Sie kannten nur die alten Rollen.

_____

8. So fing für die Gerbers ein neues Leben an.

_____

E. Reise nach Italien. While Susi's first trip to Italy was fun, it wasn't a total success. Tell about her observations by rewriting each sentence in the simple past tense.

1. In Italien scheint die Sonne immer.

_____

2. Sie geht viel schwimmen.

_____

3. Sie trinkt viel Rotwein.

_____

4. Sie ißt jeden Tag Spaghetti.

_____

5. Sie kann sonst nichts bestellen.

_____

6. Sie versteht die Menschen nicht.

_____

7. Sie bleibt zwei Tage in Rom.

_____

8. Sie will nicht länger bleiben.

_____

9. Jeden Tag schreibt sie eine Karte nach Hause.

_____

10. Sie findet es furchtbar, daß die Autos so schnell fahren.

_____

F. An der Uni. Describe Robert's experiences as a student in the Federal Republic of Germany. Use the simple past tense forms of the verbs in parentheses.

1. Während Robert an einer deutschen Universität _____,

   _____ er in einem Studentenheim. (studieren, wohnen)

2. Als er wieder nach Hause _____, _____ er seiner

   Familie, wie es in Deutschland auf der Uni _____ (kommen, erzählen,

   sein)

3. Die Universität _____ nichts. (kosten)

4. Viele Studenten _____ Geld vom Staat. (bekommen)

5. Die Studenten _____ nur ein oder zwei Fächer studieren. (müssen)

6. Sie _____ nicht jedes Semester ein Examen. (machen)

7. Das _____ Robert sehr. (gefallen)

G. Samstagabend. Michael couldn't join you at the movies, but he did make it later to the pub. Complete each sentence, using the guidelines to construct a clause or sentence in the past perfect tense.

➤ (Film / anfangen / schon), als wir ankamen.
Der Film hatte schon angefangen, als wir ankamen.

1. (Karin / sehen / Film / gestern)

_____

2. (Michael / kommen / nicht), weil er arbeiten mußte.

_____

3. (er / schreiben / sein Referat / noch nicht)

_____

4. (wir / hören / das / schon), bevor° er uns davon erzählte. | *before*

_____

5. (nachdem / wir / helfen / Michael), konnte er mit in eine Kneipe.

_____

H. Das Rad. Petra has written about the use of bicycles in the Federal Republic of Germany. Combine the sentences using **als, wann,** or **wenn,** as appropriate.

1. Ich war in Deutschland. Es gab einen Fahrradboom.

_____

2. Ich weiß nicht. Der Boom hat angefangen.

_____

3. Man fuhr mit dem Rad. Man mußte in die Stadt.

_____

4. Niemand sah mich merkwürdig an. Ich fuhr einmal mit dem Rad zum Einkaufen.

_____

© 1988 by Houghton Mifflin Company   *Kapitel 10   109*

5. Ich fuhr immer mit. Meine Freunde machten eine Radtour.

_____

6. Am Freitag fragte ich sie immer. Wir sollten uns am Sonntag treffen.

_____

I. Landeskunde. Provide brief responses in English.

1. Identify two ways in which women and men have not yet attained true equality in the workforce or in academia in the Federal Republic of Germany.

_____

_____

2. Describe two benefits established by the Federal Republic of Germany to aid parents. Do similar benefits exist in your country?

_____

_____

_____

J. Hausmann sein. Mr. Weiß is a programmer and Mrs. Weiß is an engineer. She had also run the household until yesterday, when Mr. Weiß assumed the household responsibilities. Take the role of Mr. Weiß and describe your first day as **Programmierer und Hausmann.** Use the simple past and include some modal verbs. Possible cues:

aufstehen (wann?); Frühstück für Familie machen; sich und Kinder anziehen; zur Arbeit fahren; in der Firma ankommen (wann?—zu spät/zu früh); wieviel Programme schreiben? (gut/schlecht gehen); Abendessen vorbereiten; abwaschen; ins Bett gehen (wann?)

Ich _____

_____

_____

_____

_____

_____

K. Frauen in Spitzenpositionen°. Read the passage and then answer the questions.

leading positions

Vor kurzer Zeit brachte eine deutsche Zeitung eine Studie° über Frauen in Spitzenpositionen in der Bundesrepublik. Die Studie wollte zeigen, wie diese Frauen sich selbst sahen, was für ein Familienleben sie führten und wie sie sich ihren Erfolg° erklärten. Man interviewte nur Frauen in traditionellen Männerberufen wie Professor, Jurist, Direktor eines Krankenhauses° und Manager in der Industrie. Diese Frauen hatten studiert und verdienten mehr als sechzigtausend Mark im Jahr. Zu dieser Zeit war die Frauenquote° in diesen Berufen weniger als zehn Prozent.

study

success

hospital

proportion of women

Die Studie fand, daß mehr als fünfzig Prozent dieser Frauen nicht verheiratet waren. Frauen mit eigenem Geschäft waren öfter verheiratet. Wenn diese Frauen ein Kind hatten, war es für sie leichter, ihr Kind mit ins Geschäft zu nehmen. Eine von ihnen sagte: „Als mein Kind noch klein war, hat es oft im Büro auf dem Schreibtisch° geschlafen." Für die meisten Angestellten° ist das natürlich unmöglich.

desk

employees

Für die meisten verheirateten Frauen kostete die Familie mehr Energie, als sie ihnen gab. Eine der Frauen meinte: „Die Frauen haben es im Beruf viel schwerer. Sie haben nicht, was für den Erfolg im Beruf sehr wichtig ist: eine Frau."

Andere Probleme waren zum Beispiel, daß einige Sekretärinnen absolut nicht für Frauen arbeiten wollten. Oder daß eine Ärztin kein Geld von ihrem Konto° bekommen konnte—die Bank wollte erst mit ihrem Mann sprechen.

account

Fast alle Frauen hielten° eine gute Ausbildung° für sehr wichtig und den Willen° zum Erfolg. Dafür mußten sie oft private Interessen aufgeben° und oft auch den Plan, eine Familie zu haben. Im Beruf suchten sie weniger das Geld und die Sicherheit°. Für sie war wichtiger, unabhängig zu sein und eine interessante Arbeit zu haben.

hielten für: considered / training

determination

give up / security

1. Auf welche Fragen wollte die Studie Antworten finden?

_____

2. Was für Frauen interviewte man?

_____

3. Wieviel Prozent Männer gab es in diesen Berufen?

_____

4. Warum war es für Frauen mit Kindern leichter, wenn sie ihr eigenes Geschäft hatten?

_____

5. Warum haben Frauen es im Beruf schwerer?

_____

6. Für wen wollten einige Sekretärinnen nicht arbeiten?

_____

7. Warum konnte die Ärztin kein Geld von ihrem Konto bekommen?

_____

8. Was mußten Frauen in Spitzenpositionen oft aufgeben?

_____

9. Was fanden sie im Beruf wichtiger und was weniger wichtig?

_____

RECHSTEINER PERSONALBERATUNG

Herausforderung für eine(n) junge(n)

Betriebswirtschafter(in)
(Uni/HSG)

die (der) in der Stabsabteilung

Planung und Organisation

eines führenden Unternehmens der Nahrungsmittelbranche mit Sitz in der nördlichen Agglomeration von Zürich ihr (sein) Können unter Beweis stellen möchte.

An interessanten, abwechslungsreichen und herausfordernden Organisationsprojekten fehlt es nicht. Sie werden für das Unternehmen und dessen Tochterbetriebe, zusammen mit einem jungen, dynamischen Team, Projekte aus den Bereichen

- **Logistik** - Lager und Vertriebsfragen im Rahmen einer grossen Reorganisation
- **Produktion** - Festlegung der Aufgabenteilung der Produktionsbetriebe
- **Controlling** - Erweiterung, Betreuung und Auswertung eines Kennzahlensystems in Logistik und anderen Bereichen

bearbeiten.

Eine faszinierende Aufgabe. Ein Angebot, das sich zu prüfen lohnt!

Setzen Sie sich mit uns in Verbindung. Wir freuen uns darauf und informieren Sie gerne über Wissenwertes und Interessantes unseres Mandanten.

Rechsteiner Personalberatung
Tramstrasse 10
8050 Zürich
Tel. (01) 311 31 11.

SOX634770K

Kapitel 11

A. Spielst du mit? Create a dialogue based on the following guidelines, using subjunctive and würde-constructions, where appropriate.

Beate: Du, Sascha / / meine Band / spielen / bei / eine Wahlveranstaltung
du / Lust haben / mitspielen / ?

_____

_____

Sascha: ich / machen / das / gern

_____

Beate: was / du / vorhaben / heute / ?

_____

Sascha: Nichts.

Beate: du / können / kommen / heute / zu / Probe / ?

_____

Sascha: ja / können / ich

_____

B. Sie haben das Wort. Respond appropriately. See Reference Sections #11 and #24 on pages R-20 and R-23 of your textbook.

Agreeing to a Request

1. *Freund/in:* Mein Auto ist kaputt. Könntest du mich morgen abholen?
   Du: _____

2. *Freund/in:* Hättest du Lust, nach dem Seminar ins Café zu gehen?
   Du: _____

Giving Advice

3. *Freund/in:* Ich weiß nicht, ob ich heute segeln gehen soll. Der Wind ist furchtbar stark.
   Du: _____

4. *Freund/in:* Bei der Probe hat Paul wieder falsch° gespielt. Sollte | *out of tune*
   ich mit ihm darüber reden?
   Du: _____

C. Verben, Verben. Give the general subjunctive forms of the following verb phrases in both present and past time.

	Present time	Past time
1. er denkt		
2. ich esse		
3. du fährst		
4. sie findet		
5. wir geben		
6. es gefällt		
7. er geht		
8. sie hält		
9. Sie bringen		
10. ihr habt		
11. wir laufen		
12. ich lese		
13. du nimmst		
14. sie schläft		
15. wir sehen		
16. ich spreche		
17. er trinkt		
18. sie tun		
19. es wird		
20. du bist		

Wer ans **ZIEL** getragen wurde, darf nicht glauben, es erreicht zu haben.

D. Schwierigkeiten. Sabine is finding it difficult to attend the entire rehearsal of her music group. Rewrite each sentence below to express politeness, using the present-time subjunctive of the modals.

➤ *Michael:* Kannst du um sieben zur Probe kommen?
Könntest du um sieben zur Probe kommen?

Sabine: Muß es um sieben sein?

_____

Michael: Die Probe soll vier Stunden dauern.

_____

Sabine: Darf ich vielleicht um acht kommen?

_____

Michael: Sicher kannst du das, aber...

_____

Sabine: Morgen kann ich um sieben kommen.

_____

E. Am Bodensee. Stephanie is on vacation at Lake Constance. She wishes conditions were different. Express her sentences as positive wishes in the subjunctive.

➤ Das Wetter ist nicht schön.   *Wenn das Wetter nur schön wäre!*

1. Die Sonne scheint nicht.

_____

2. Ich kann nicht windsurfen gehen.

_____

3. Es gibt kein Fest hier.

_____

4. Ich habe zuwenig Geld. (use *mehr*)

_____

5. Kurt ist nicht mitgekommen.

_____

6. Er hat nicht geschrieben.

_____

F. Wenn...dann. Provide conclusions for the conditional sentences below, telling what you might do or might have done during a holiday or leisure time.

1. Wenn heute Silvester wäre, _____

_____

2. Wenn ich abends nicht arbeiten müßte, _____

_____

3. Wenn wir im Juli am Bodensee gewesen wären, _____

_____

4. Wenn ich letzten Sommer mehr Zeit/Geld gehabt hätte, _____

_____

G. Wenn wir das anders gemacht hätten... Klaus and members of his **WG** discuss how things might have been. Restate the sentences below using the past-time subjunctive of the modal.

➤ Ich müßte nicht immer kochen.
Ich hätte nicht immer kochen müssen.

1. Wir müßten nicht immer Spaghetti essen.

_____

2. Bernd könnte bei der Hausarbeit helfen.

_____

3. Thomas dürfte nicht immer so lange schlafen.

_____

4. Du müßtest die Küche nicht so oft saubermachen.

_____

5. Wir könnten zusammen ins Theater gehen.

_____

6. Ich sollte die Nachbarn zum Picknick einladen.

_____

H. Freizeit ein Problem? Read the passage and then answer the questions.

„Alle gingen in ihr Zimmer, machten die Tür zu und taten eine oder
eineinhalb Stunden, was sie wollten. Unsere eine Tochter wollte Musik
hören. Unsere andere Tochter wollte fernsehen. Meine Frau wollte
lesen. Ich wollte etwas schlafen. So haben wir alle einen sehr
schönen Sonntagnachmittag verbracht", erzählt Dr. Feldgen vom Institut
für Freizeitforschung° in Hamburg.　　　　　　　　　　　　　　　　| *research on leisure*

Man möchte fragen: „Ja und? Ist das etwas Besonderes?" Nach Dr.
Feldgen, ja. Viele Leute finden nämlich, daß Freizeit ein Problem
ist, wenn auch nur wenige darüber sprechen. Typisch ist z.B., wenn
eine Frau sagt: „Erst hat mein Mann ein Fußballspiel angesehen. Dann
hat er gesagt, er muß arbeiten. Und ich wäre so gern mit ihm
spazierengegangen. Für mich hat er aber wieder mal keine Zeit
gehabt." Oder ein Mann sagt: „Meine Frau und meine Kinder wollten
letzten Sonntag absolut mit mir ins Museum. Und ich hätte so gern
allein in meinem Zimmer gesessen und endlich mein neues Buch gelesen."

In den meisten Familien wollen die Menschen vor allem zwei Dinge.
Sie wollen Kontakt mit anderen, wollen etwas zusammen machen. Sie
wollen aber auch allein sein, weg von den anderen. In diesem
Dilemma ist Fernsehen oft der einzige Ausweg°. Man weiß nicht,　　　| *way out*
was man machen soll. So sieht man eben fern. Wenn der Fernseher
kaputt ist, gibt's eine Familienkrise°.　　　　　　　　　　　　　　| *family crisis*

Für viele ist Freizeit keine freie Zeit. Am Wochenende sagen sie
sich: Ich müßte eigentlich die Fenster putzen; ich sollte eigentlich
die Garage aufräumen; ich könnte eigentlich im Garten arbeiten usw.
Für diese Aktivitäten gibt man seine freie Zeit auf°. Oder man macht　| *gibt...auf: gives up*
einen großen Plan für die ganze Familie. Dieser Plan soll dann
alle in der Familie zufriedenstellen°. Statt Zufriedenheit° gibt's　　| *satisfy / satisfac-*
aber oft Unzufriedenheit, Frustration, Aggression, Streß.　　　　　　| *tion*

Für viele ist Freitag der schönste Tag der Woche. Man denkt
daran, was man am Wochenende gern machen würde. Die Wirklichkeit
ist dann aber oft gar nicht so schön. Warum? Dr. Feldgen sagt: „Weil
wir nicht gelernt haben, was wir brauchen. Wir brauchen freie Zeit
für persönliche Wünsche°. Wir brauchen freie Zeit für Kontakt mit　　| *wishes*
anderen. Und wir brauchen freie Zeit, nichts zu tun, ohne
Langeweile° und ohne Schuldgefühle°.　　　　　　　　　　　　　　| *boredom / feelings*
　　　　　　　　　　　　　　　　　　　　　　　　　　　　　　| *of guilt*

1. Warum war der Sonntagnachmittag für alle in Dr. Feldgens Familie sehr schön?

_____

2. Warum ist ein schöner Sonntagnachmittag für alle in der Familie etwas Besonderes?

_____

　　　　　　　　　　　　　　　　　　　Kapitel 11　　117

3. Was hätte die Frau gern gemacht?

_____

4. Was hätte der Mann gern gemacht?

_____

5. Was wollen die Menschen in den meisten Familien?

_____

6. Warum sehen viele Menschen am Wochenende oft fern?

_____

7. Was machen viele Leute am Wochenende?

_____

8. Warum ist für viele Freitag der schönste Tag der Woche?

_____

I. Landeskunde. Provide brief responses in English.

1. Compare theaters in German-speaking countries with those in your community in terms of their repertoires and jurisdiction (e.g., city or state theaters? private theaters?).

_____

_____

2. Name two facts which you find interesting about Bach, Mozart, or Beethoven. Which composer's works do you or might you enjoy hearing?

_____

_____

_____

J. Das Freizeit-Budget. Use the information given in the table below to answer the following questions on leisure time in the Federal Republic of Germany.

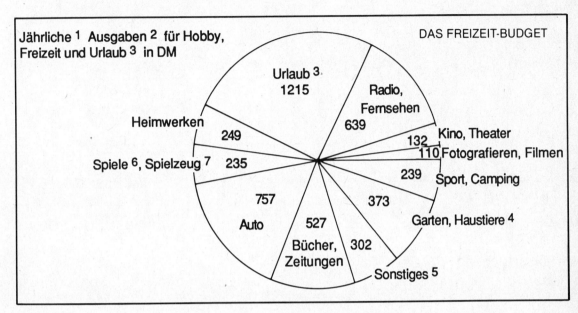

Jährliche [1] Ausgaben [2] für Hobby, Freizeit und Urlaub [3] in DM

DAS FREIZEIT-BUDGET

Urlaub [3] 1215

Radio, Fernsehen 639

Kino, Theater 132

Fotografieren, Filmen 110

Sport, Camping 239

Garten, Haustiere [4] 373

Sonstiges [5] 302

Bücher, Zeitungen 527

Auto 757

Spiele [6], Spielzeug [7] 235

Heimwerken 249

[1] annual	[2] expenditures	[3] *der Urlaub*: vacation	[4] pets
[5] other	[6] games	[7] toys	

1. Für welche Freizeitbeschäftigung° geben die Deutschen am meisten aus°? | *leisure activity / geben...aus: spend*

_____

2. Wofür geben sie mehr aus—für Fernsehen und Radio oder für Bücher und Zeitungen?

_____

3. Von den drei Hobbys—Garten, Sport und Heimwerken°—welches ist | *do-it-yourself projects*
   am populärsten? Welches steht an zweiter Stelle und welches an dritter
   Stelle?

_____

_____

K. Familie, Arbeit, Freizeit. Answer each of the following personalized questions with a complete sentence.

1. Als Sie noch klein waren, wer hat für Sie gesorgt? Immer? Manchmal?

_____

2. Wer hat außerhalb des Hauses gearbeitet?

_____

3. Was hat Ihre Familie in der Freizeit gemacht?

_____

4. Wenn Sie eines Tages heiraten°, wer wird den Haushalt machen?　　| *marry*
   Wenn Sie schon verheiratet° sind, wer macht den Haushalt?　　| *married*

_____

5. Wer verdient das Geld?

_____

6. Was sind Ihre Hobbys?

_____

7. Wenn Sie andere Hobbys haben könnten, was würden Sie gern machen?

_____

8. Wenn Sie etwas in Ihrem Lebensstil° ändern° wollten und könnten,　　| *lifestyle / change*
   was für Änderungen würden Sie machen?

_____

Urlaub auf dem Bauernhof

　　　　　　　　© *1988 by Houghton Mifflin Company*

Kapitel 12

A. Eine Frage der Qualität. Ms. Meister is trying to sell a previous customer her company's new computer. In a short German paragraph, write a summary of what happened at a recent meeting.

Frau Meister: So, Herr Kohl, was halten Sie von unseren Preisen?

Herr Kohl: Sie wissen, es ist keine Frage des Preises. Ihre Computer sind nicht gerade billig, aber darüber können wir später reden. Am wichtigsten ist die Frage der Qualität.

Frau Meister: Bei unserem Namen, Herr Kohl? „Solo" ist in der ganzen Welt bekannt.

Herr Kohl: Trotzdem. Die Computer, die wir vor fünf Jahren bei Ihnen gekauft haben, haben wir ziemlich oft reparieren müssen.

Frau Meister: Leider. Aber die Bildprobleme sind jetzt gelöst. Der neue Solo Personal Computer 90 arbeitet auch schneller. Sie werden also viel Zeit sparen°. Außerdem kann man mit unserem Software-Packet ohne Programmierer programmieren. Sie brauchen kein kompliziertes Programm zu schreiben, Sie brauchen nur ein paar Worte zu tippen°. Ich bin sicher, Sie werden zufrieden° sein. | *save* | *type* | *satisfied*

Herr Kohl: Hm, ja.... Wir werden uns in den nächsten Tagen entscheiden. Ich kann Sie am Montag in einer Woche wissen lassen, ob wir den „Solo" kaufen wollen. Dann können wir noch einmal über die Preise reden, nicht?

_____

_____

_____

_____

_____

B. Sie haben das Wort. Respond appropriately. See Reference Sections #21 and #25 on pages R-22 and R-23 of your textbook.

Making Surmises

1. *Kollegin:* Bringt Frau Richter eine Preisliste mit?

   Du: _____

2. *Kollege:* Ich habe gehört, wir kaufen dreißig neue Solo Computer.

   Du: _____

3. *Freund/in:* Glaubst du wirklich, ich verdiene zuviel?

   Du: _____

4. *Freund/in:* Willst du damit sagen, ich arbeite zuwenig?

   Du: _____

C. Wofür gibt man sein Geld aus°? In the Federal Republic of Germany, | *gibt...aus: spend*
four hundred selected families with monthly disposable incomes of 3,600
marks keep detailed accounts of all their monthly expenses. Write out
each fraction in the statements below.

1. Jeden Monat gibt man _____ des
   Geldes für Essen und Miete° aus. (1/3) | *rent*

2. Man gibt _____ des Geldes
   für Auto und Fahrgeld° aus. (1/8) | *bus fares, etc.*

3. Man gibt _____ des Geldes
   für Kleidung und Schuhe aus. (1/13)

4. _____ des Geldes gibt man jeden Monat
   für Möbel und für den Haushalt aus. (1/16)

5. _____ des Geldes gibt man
   für Essen, Miete, Auto, Elektrizität und Heizung° aus. (1/2) | *home heating*

D. Neue Stellen. Manfred is telling Peter about his and Karin's plans for new jobs. Rewrite his
sentences in the future tense.

1. Ich nehme einen Informatik-Kurs.

   _____

2. Hilfst du mir?

   _____

3. Wir können abends arbeiten, nicht?

   _____

4. Karin sucht einen neuen Job.

   _____

5. Ich glaube, daß eine andere Stelle ihr besser gefällt. (*do not change* **ich glaube**)

   _____

6. Wir müssen die Hausarbeit samstags machen.

   _____

E. So war es möglich. Mrs. Wieland explains how she was able to work full time and raise three children. Give the English equivalents of her sentences.

1. Die Kinder sagten oft: „Laß uns dies oder das machen!"

_____

2. Ich habe die Kinder immer abwaschen lassen.

_____

3. Wir haben auch viel Arbeit einfach liegenlassen.

_____

4. Wir haben den Kindern immer genug Zeit gelassen, ihre Schulaufgaben zu machen.

_____

5. Als die Kinder jung waren, haben wir sie nicht allein gelassen.

_____

6. Wir haben immer einen Babysitter kommen lassen.

_____

F. Relativpronomen. Complete the following definitions by supplying the relative pronouns.

1. Eine Frau, _____ aus Deutschland kommt, ist eine Deutsche.

2. Ein junger Mann, _____ an einer Universität studiert, ist ein Student.

3. Das Essen, _____ man zu Abend ißt, ist das Abendessen.

4. Leute, für _____ man arbeitet, sind Chefs oder Chefinnen.

5. Ein Geschäft, in _____ man Brot kauft, ist eine Bäckerei.

6. Ein Instrument, mit _____ man Musik machen kann, ist ein Musikinstrument.

G. Schreiben Sie Definitionen! Now write your own definitions, using relative clauses.

1. Bäcker _____

2. Buchhandlung _____

3. Schlafzimmer _____

4. Waschmaschine _____

H. Unterschiede. Claudia and Robert are discussing differences they noted between German and American culture. Complete the sentences with a relative clause, using the guidelines.

➤ Claudia spricht mit einem Freund, (sie hat ihn in Deutschland kennengelernt).
Claudia spricht mit einem Freund, den sie in Deutschland kennengelernt hat.

1. Sie sprechen über kulturelle Unterschiede, (sie haben die Unterschiede bemerkt).

_____

2. Die Fahrer, (die Fahrer hat Robert in Deutschland gesehen), sind wie die Wilden gefahren.

_____

_____

3. Die Züge, (er ist mit den Zügen gefahren), waren meistens pünktlich.

_____

4. Einen Flur, (der Flur wäre für eine deutsche Wohnung typisch), hat Claudias amerikanische Wohnung nicht.

_____

5. Claudia hat Hunger auf Brot, (das Brot ist schwerer als amerikanisches Brot).

_____

6. Sie hat auch Hunger auf den Kuchen, (sie hat von dem Kuchen in Bonn immer drei Stücke gegessen).

_____

Intercity. Jede Stunde.
Jede Klasse.

Deutsche
Bundesbahn

Wie Ihr Fahrrad mit der
Bahn in den Urlaub fährt.

Deutsche
Bundesbahn

I. Arbeitsorganisation—Experimente in der Industrie. Read the passage and then answer the questions.

Vielleicht wird die Mitbestimmung° die Entfremdung° des modernen Industriearbeiters mildern°. Vielleicht wird man da aber noch ganz andere Konzepte brauchen, wie man sie in Schweden versucht: Gruppenarbeit statt Fließbandarbeit°, Variation statt Monotonie, Konsultation der Arbeiter statt Kontrolle. | *codetermination / alienation | alleviate* | *assembly line work*

In der schwedischen Autoindustrie hatte man bemerkt, daß viele Arbeiterinnen nach kurzer Zeit mit der Arbeit aufhörten, daß sie oft wegen Krankheit nicht zur Arbeit kamen, daß es schwer war, neue Arbeiterinnen zu finden und daß die Arbeitsqualität oft nicht sehr gut war. Man mußte also versuchen, die Arbeit attraktiver zu machen.

Eine Autofirma ließ daher ein Experiment machen. *Mit* den Arbeiterinnen, nicht *für* sie plante man eine neue Arbeitsorganisation. Die Frauen arbeiteten von jetzt an in kleinen Gruppen, die so organisiert waren, daß die Kolleginnen viel Kontakt miteinander hatten. Jede Gruppe war voll° für ein Produkt verantwortlich°. | *fully / responsible*

Das Fließband hatte den Frauen für jede Arbeit maximal 1,8 Minuten gelassen. Jetzt produzierten sie als Gruppe einen kompletten Motor in dreißig Minuten. Man ließ jede Gruppe von drei oder vier Frauen die Arbeit so organisieren, wie sie wollte. Sie konnten zusammen montieren° oder allein. Die meisten wollten lieber einen kompletten Motor allein montieren. Sie fanden das interessanter und waren so unabhängiger. Wenn sie weniger Zeit brauchten, konnten sie eine Pause machen oder mit Freunden oder Kindern telefonieren. | *assemble*

Das Experiment hatte gute Resultate: weniger Arbeiterinnen, die mit der Arbeit aufhörten; weniger Arbeiterinnen, die wegen Krankheit zu Hause blieben. Man fand, daß die Frauen aus den Gruppen, die gut funktionierten, überhaupt nicht zu Hause bleiben wollten. Sie fühlten sich für die Kolleginnen, mit denen sie zusammen arbeiteten, verantwortlich. Schließlich wurde auch die Qualität der Produkte besser, weil kleine Gruppen für ganz bestimmte Motoren verantwortlich waren.

1. Warum mußte man versuchen, die Arbeit attraktiver zu machen? Nennen Sie zwei Gründe!

_____

_____

2. Warum arbeiteten die Frauen wohl in kleinen Gruppen von drei bis vier Personen? Was meinen Sie?

_____

_____

3. Wofür war jede Gruppe verantwortlich?

_____

4. Warum wollten die meisten ihre Motoren allein montieren?

_____

5. Was konnten sie mit der Zeit, die sie übrig° hatten, machen? | *left over*

_____

_____

6. Welche Resultate hatte das Experiment?

_____

_____

7. Welche Unterschiede sehen Sie zwischen traditioneller Fließbandarbeit und der Arbeit in der schwedischen Autofirma?

_____

_____

8. Möchten Sie Fließbandarbeit machen? Warum (nicht)?

_____

_____

J. Große Pläne. Imagine you are a West German politician. Write a brief campaign statement in which you identify a problem concerning **Wirtschaft, Handel, Lebensstandard,** or **Arbeitslosigkeit.** Tell what you believe must be done, and what you will do.

_____

_____

_____

_____

_____

K. Landeskunde. Provide brief responses in English.

1. Explain the term "codetermination." Does your country have such a policy?

_____

_____

2. Describe how young Germans prepare themselves for a skilled career in industry or business.

_____

_____

3. What measures were taken after World War II to stop inflation in the Federal Republic of Germany?

_____

_____

4. For which social legislation in the Federal Republic of Germany does your country have parallel legislation, and for which does it not? Give two examples for each.

_____

_____

Kapitel 13

A. Gespräch mit Rita. You feel like going to a movie. Discuss your plans with Rita in German. Use the following guidelines.

1. Ask if she feels like going to the movies tonight.

_____

2. Rita says she's broke, and asks if you could lend her some money.

_____

_____

3. You agree.

_____

4. She asks what you would like to see.

_____

5. Tell her the name of the movie. Tell her it's a movie with (...name of actor/actress) and (...).

_____

6. Rita says that would interest her.

_____

B. Sie haben das Wort. Respond appropriately. For additional responses see Reference Sections #16 and #22 on pages R-21 and R-22 of your textbook.

Expressing Rejection

1. *Freund/in:* Ich habe zwei Karten für *Das Leben des Galilei.* Willst du mit?
   Du: _____

2. *Freund/in:* Die Filmschauspielerin° Katharina Koch ist spitze, nicht? | *actress*
   Du: _____

Expressing Expectation

3. *Freund/in:* Du kommst mit ins Theater, nicht?
   Du: _____

4. *Freund/in:* Ich bin froh, daß wir Karten für das Open-Air-Konzert bekommen haben. Es soll sehr gut sein.
   Du: _____

C. Reise in die DDR. Tell about a journalist's trip to the **DDR**. Rewrite each sentence in the tense given in parentheses.

1. Die Reise durch die DDR wird von der Journalistin im Herbst gemacht. (*simple past*)

_____

2. Die Journalistin wird durch einige Fabriken° geführt. (*simple past*) | *factories*

_____

3. Voll berufstätigen Frauen mit Kindern wurde vom Staat geholfen. (*present*)

_____

4. In der Industrie wurde überall etwa gleich viel verdient. (*present*)

_____

5. Über die negative Seite wird nichts gesagt. (*simple past*)

_____

D. Das Verb *werden*. Complete each sentence with the appropriate form of **werden**. Then give the English equivalent of the sentence.

1. Am Nachmittag _____ (past) das Wetter immer schlechter.

_____

2. Karla ist letzte Woche krank _____.

_____

3. _____ du dein Rad verkaufen?

_____

4. Was muß noch getan _____?

_____

5. Er _____ wohl noch heute kommen.

_____

6. Was möchte Renate _____? Journalistin?

_____

7. Kann das Auto so schnell repariert _____?

_____

8. Der Brief _____ heute geschrieben.

_____

E. Lebensstandard in der DDR. Bärbel has made notes for a report on the standard of living in the **DDR**. Rewrite her sentences in the active voice, using **man**.

➤ Der Lebensstandard wurde mit anderen Ostblockstaaten verglichen.
Man verglich den Lebensstandard mit anderen Ostblockstaaten.

1. Ein hoher Lebensstandard wird erwartet.

_____

2. In den letzten Jahren sind viele Autos bestellt worden.

_____

3. Viele Arbeiter werden durch Computer ersetzt werden.

_____

4. Neue Jobs müssen gefunden werden.

_____

5. Die Probleme der Rentner° können nicht leicht gelöst werden. | *pensioners*

_____

F. Lebensstandard in der Bundesrepublik. Martin also has notes on the economic situation in the Federal Republic of Germany. Rewrite his sentences, using **sein + zu +** infinitive, with the original object as the new subject.

➤ Man kann den hohen Lebensstandard leicht erklären.
Der hohe Lebensstandard ist leicht zu erklären.

1. Qualitätsprodukte kann man leichter verkaufen.

_____

2. Die wichtige Rolle des Exports kann man leicht verstehen.

_____

3. Die Inflationsrate muß man so niedrig wie möglich halten.

_____

4. Die geographischen Fakten kann man nicht ändern.

_____

5. Probleme der Arbeitslosigkeit kann man im Moment kaum lösen.

_____

G. Natürlichkeit. Richard intends to write a report on the Germans' interest in natural living. Below are his notes. Restate them, using a reflexive construction.

➤ Es ist besser da zu leben, wo die Luft rein ist.
Es lebt sich besser da, wo die Luft rein ist.

1. Die vielen Reklamen mit dem Wort „Natur" sind leicht zu erklären.

_____

2. Natürliche Lebensmittel sind leicht zu verkaufen.

_____

3. Es ist besser, bei geöffnetem Fenster zu schlafen.

_____

4. Es ist schöner, an einem sauberen See zu sitzen.

_____

5. Ein Tisch aus Holz° ist leichter zu reparieren als ein Tisch aus Plastik. | *wood*

_____

H. Etwas Neues. Inge assures Petra that she can handle the new responsibilities at work. Answer Petra's questions, using a form of **sich lassen** + infinitive.

➤ Kann man die Programmiersprache wirklich lernen?
Ja, die Programmiersprache läßt sich wirklich lernen.

1. Kann man das in zwei Monaten machen?

_____

2. Kann man Bücher über die neue Sprache finden?

_____

3. Kann man die Bücher leicht lesen?

_____

4. Kann man mit den Lehrern gut arbeiten?

_____

5. Kann man mit ihnen offen reden?

_____

I. Freizeit. Holger wants to know about leisure time in a student's life. He writes to his friend Cornelia. Complete the sentences with an appropriate preposition. To review verbs and prepositions with special meanings, see Reference Section #16, page R-12, and page 253.

Holger hat _____ seine Freundin Cornelia geschrieben. Sie studiert

_____ der Universität Leipzig. Er möchte etwas _____ Freizeit

_____ der Uni wissen. Cornelia antwortet, daß, was ein Student in der Freizeit

macht, _____ dem Studenten abhängt. Sie erzählt _____ ihren

Freunden. Ihre Freundin Gabi, zum Beispiel, fängt immer früh _____ ihrer Arbeit

an, denn abends macht sie _____ einer Musikgruppe mit. Ihr Freund Jan interessiert

sich _____ Fußball. Er geht auch abends viel _____ eine Gaststätte, wo

er _____ seine Freunde wartet. Sie hören gern Jazz. Sie halten besonders viel

_____ zwei Gruppen aus Halle. Cornelias Freundin Silke fotografiert gern. Ihre

Bilder werden manchmal _____ einer Zeitschrift gekauft. _____ ihre

Bilder verdient sie genug für ihre Ferien.

J. Muß es denn gerade eine Frau aus dem Westen sein? Read the passage and then answer the questions.

Erik Bunge aus Berlin (Ost) hatte eine Frau aus der Bundesrepublik kennengelernt. Es war die große Liebe°. Die beiden wollten heiraten°. Das Problem war nur: Wie konnte Erik legal in den Westen? | *love / marry*

Das Problem scheint überhaupt kein Problem zu sein. Hat nicht nach Helsinki° jeder Mensch das Recht, in dem Land zu leben, in dem er leben will? Ja, aber für viele Sozialisten ist es ein unmöglicher Gedanke°, daß jemand in einem kapitalistischen Land leben will. Oder es sollte doch ein unmöglicher Gedanke sein, meinen sie. | *Helsinki accord* | *thought*

Erik Bunge war Student an einer Ingenieurschule. Er war in der FDJ, der Freien Deutschen Jugend, der staatlichen Jugendorganisation, aktiv. Er machte gerade bei einer Firma in Berlin (Ost) sein Praktikum°, als er beantragte°, in den Westen gehen zu dürfen. Zwei Tage danach wurde er exmatrikuliert° und verlor Arbeit und Zimmer. Der Direktor der Ingenieurschule fuhr zu seinen Eltern. Die Eltern sollten den Sohn beeinflussen. Erik ließ sich aber nicht beeinflussen. Er wollte zu seiner Inge. | *internship* | *applied* | *expelled*

Lange Zeit hörte Erik nun nichts. Ein neues Zimmer mußte also gefunden werden. Das war schwer. Eine neue Stelle war überhaupt nicht zu finden. Er fand mehrere freie Stellen. Aber wenn man hörte, daß er beantragt hatte, in den Westen zu gehen, kamen Antworten wie: „Es tut uns leid, aber die Stelle ist doch nicht frei." Oder: „Es ist eine Frage der Qualifikationen. Bei uns werden doch etwas andere

Qualifikationen gebraucht." In *einer* Firma sagte man ihm ganz offen:
„Leute, die in den Westen wollen, können hier nicht einmal° als
Hilfsarbeiter° gebraucht werden."

*nicht einmal: not
even / unskilled
worker*

   Kein Mensch schien zu wissen, wann er eine Antwort erwarten
konnte. Einige Leute hatten nach kurzer Zeit eine Antwort bekommen.
Bei anderen wieder war es sehr langsam gegangen. Waren diese
Unterschiede nun Teil des politischen Systems, oder war es einfach
die Schlamperei° der Bürokratie? Es war schwer zu sagen.

bungling

   Eines Nachmittags mußte es dann plötzlich sehr schnell gehen. Er mußte
in drei Stunden reisefertig sein. Daher hat er immer noch Sachen
bei seinen Eltern. Er hatte keine Zeit, zu ihnen zu fahren. Er will
sie in ein paar Monaten mit seiner Frau besuchen.

1. Wo war Erik Bunge zu Hause?

_____

2. Warum konnte er Inge nicht einfach heiraten?

_____

3. Welches Recht sollte nach Helsinki jeder Mensch haben?

_____

4. Warum können Menschen aus der DDR nicht einfach in den Westen gehen?

_____

5. Was war Erik Bunge von Beruf?

_____

6. Warum fuhr der Direktor zu seinen Eltern?

_____

7. Warum konnte Erik keine Arbeit finden?

_____

8. Warum hat er immer noch Sachen bei seinen Eltern?

_____

K. Landeskunde. Provide brief responses in English.

1. Identify an aspect of public school education in the DDR that differs from policies in your country.

_____

_____

2. Explain Berlin's special status in theoretical terms and in terms of its location.

_____

_____

L. Identifizieren Sie! Identify the three regions of mountains (**Gebirge**) and woods and the twelve institutions of higher education marked on the map of the German Democratic Republic. Refer to the map on the inside cover of your textbook as necessary.

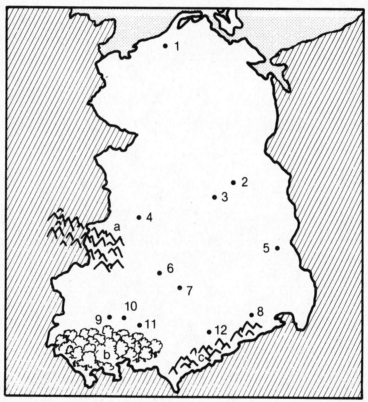

Gebirge und Wälder:

_____ Erzgebirge   _____ Harz   _____ Thüringer Wald

Universitäten, Hochschulen, Akademien:

_____ Humboldt-Universität, Berlin (Ost)

_____ Ingenieurhochschule Cottbus

_____ Technische Universität Dresden

_____ Medizinische Akademie Erfurt

_____ Pädagogische Hochschule „Nadeshda Konstantinowna Krupskaja", Halle

_____ Friedrich-Schiller-Universität, Jena

_____ Technische Hochschule Karl-Marx-Stadt

_____ Theaterhochschule „Hans Otto", Leipzig

_____ Medizinische Akademie Magdeburg

_____ Pädagogische Hochschule „Karl Liebknecht", Potsdam

_____ Universität Rostock

_____ Hochschule für Musik „Franz Liszt", Weimar

M. Extra-Übung: Kreuzworträtsel°.

crossword puzzle

Waagerecht

2. known
5. when
7. names
8. greet, as in ___ dich!
10. part
12. (you) do
13. (he) sang
16. city
18. older
19. one

Senkrecht

1. trains
2. trade union
3. (you) know
4. drink! (fam.)
6. noses
9. something
11. wage
14. eye
15. green
17. door

Kapitel 14

A. Der Zeitungsartikel. Tell Stefan, a German exchange student, about some things you have read in today's paper. Give the German equivalents of the following statements, supplying the missing information on the current economic situation in your country.

1. Have you seen the paper today?

_____

2. I read that we have (high? low?) unemployment.

_____

3. Did you know that we still have (?) percent unemployment?

_____

4. Have you heard there's a strike at (?)?

_____

5. Did you know that the government is talking about a tax (increase? decrease?)?

_____

6. I read that new houses are selling (well? poorly?). (Use reflexive for **daß**-clause.)

_____

B. Sie haben das Wort. Respond appropriately. For additional expressions see Reference Sections #18 and #19 on pages R-21 and R-22 of your textbook.

Expressing Sadness

1. *Freund/in:* Hast du schon gehört, daß Herr Meier seine Stelle verloren hat?
   Du: _____
2. *Freund/in:* Hast du schon gehört? Alis Eltern wollen zurück in die Türkei. Er soll mit.
   Du: _____

Making Requests

3. *Du:* Ich will am Freitag ins Konzert.

_____

   Freund/in: Ja, klar!
4. *Du:* Ich wollte Ingrid und Peter auch einladen.

_____

   Freund/in: Natürlich nicht.

C. Eine Lösung. Petra is thinking of giving up her career because of her new baby. Tell about her discussion with Ursel. Rewrite as indirect quotations, using general subjunctive.

1. Petra sagte: „Ich habe schon drei Jahre gearbeitet."

   Petra sagte, sie _____

2. Sie sagte: „Die Arbeit gefällt mir."

   Sie sagte, die Arbeit _____

3. Ursel fragte: „Warum willst du dann aufhören?"

   Ursel fragte, warum sie _____

4. Ursel sagte: „Tu das nicht!"

   Ursel sagte, daß sie _____

5. Petra fragte: „Wer wird für das Kind sorgen?"

   Petra fragte, wer _____

6. Ursel fragte: „Kann dein Mann nicht zu Hause mehr helfen?"

   Ursel fragte, ob ihr Mann _____

7. Petra sagte: „Er hat das schon angeboten."

   Petra sagte, daß er _____

8. Ursel sagte: „Dann sehe ich wirklich kein Problem mehr."

   Ursel sagte, sie _____

D. Keine Zeit. Read Monika's end of a telephone conversation. Then retell it in narrative form, using the general subjunctive in indirect discourse.

Hallo! ... Wer ist da? ... Ach, guten Tag, Klaus! ... Was ich heute abend mache? ... Mit dir ins Kino? Leider kann ich nicht. Ich sehe heute abend fern. Um 21 Uhr gibt es eine besonders interessante Sendung ... Am Wochenende fahre ich mit Karin und Trudi an den See. Wir kommen erst Sonntag abend wieder nach Hause ... Montag singe ich in einem Konzert ... Nein, am Dienstag gehe ich ins Theater ... Aber ich habe meine Karte schon vor einem Monat gekauft! ... Nein, heute in einer Woche muß ich Wäsche waschen ... Nein, ich werde meine Großeltern besuchen ... Hallo? ... Hallo?

Leider konnte Monika nicht mit Klaus ins Kino. Sie sagte, sie _____

_____

_____

_____

_____

_____

DER STROM IST WEG, ICH MUSS DEN ELEKTRIKER ANRUFEN!

WER WOHL GEWONNEN HAT? WAR DAS UNSERE BOMBE?

...UND DAS IST ERST DER ANFANG. IM KINO GEHT'S WEITER !!

JETZT IM KINO   WELLENBERG

E. Verben. Complete the chart, using **sie/er** as the implied subject.

Present	General Subjunctive (present time)	Special Subjunctive (present time)
1. vergleicht	_____	_____
2. verspricht	_____	_____
3. fängt an	_____	_____
4. hält	_____	_____
5. weiß	_____	_____
6. ist	_____	_____
7. denkt	_____	_____
8. findet	_____	_____
9. läßt	_____	_____
10. entscheidet	_____	_____

F. Entschuldigungen. Herr Arnim invited several people to attend a meeting with him, but no one is able to go. Rewrite their messages in the general subjunctive.

1. Herr Jacobs hat gesagt, er komme leider nicht mit.

_____

2. Frau Stern hat gesagt, sie rufe nächste Woche an.

_____

3. Herr Neis hat gesagt, das gehe heute nicht.

_____

4. Herr Haas hat gesagt, er müsse nach Bonn.

_____

5. Frau Meier hat gesagt, Frau Busch könne mitgehen.

_____

6. Frau Busch hat gesagt, sie habe schon etwas vor.

_____

7. Herr Stein hat gesagt, Herr Kraus sei nach Bern gefahren.

_____

8. Herr Schulz hat gesagt, er werde später mit ihm telefonieren.

_____

G. Landeskunde. Provide brief responses in English.

1. Name three concerns the Federal Republic of Germany faces with regard to its **Ausländer** population.

_____

_____

_____

2. Compare problems faced by foreigners living in the Federal Republic of Germany with problems faced by foreign exchange students or immigrants in your community. Identify at least one similarity and one difference.

_____

_____

H. Schreiben Sie! Write definitions in German for the following words.

1. ausländisch _____

_____

2. arbeitslos _____

_____

3. streiken _____

_____

4. die Heimat _____

_____

5. Gastarbeiter _____

_____

© 1988 by Houghton Mifflin Company

I. Brief aus Deutschland. Sue is an American living in Germany and working in a factory in Berlin. Read her letter to her former German instructor and then answer the questions.

Berlin, den 5. Mai

Liebe° Frau Hill! | *dear*

Ich danke Ihnen für Ihren freundlichen Brief. Es geht mir gut.
Mein Deutsch wird langsam besser, aber leider eben nur langsam.
Wenn ich abends aus der Fabrik° nach Hause komme, bin ich | *factory*
müde. Und in der Fabrik habe ich viel Kontakt zu Türkinnen, die
kein oder wenig Deutsch können.

Da ich mehr Deutsch kann als die Türkinnen, aber natürlich weniger
als die Deutschen, stehe ich ein bißchen zwischen beiden Gruppen.
Ich kann gut verstehen, warum die Türkinnen Schwierigkeiten mit
Deutsch haben. Ich sehe, wie schwer es ist, Deutsch zu lernen, wenn
man den ganzen Tag mit Türkinnen zusammen ist. Für manche von
ihnen kommt noch dazu, daß sie die eigene Sprache nur sprechen, aber
nicht lesen und schreiben können. Die deutschen Kolleginnen sehen aber
nur, daß so viele Türkinnen kein oder wenig Deutsch können. Ich habe
von den Deutschen daher oft gehört, daß die Ausländer eben nicht
wirklich versuchten, Deutsch zu lernen. Wirkliche Gespräche mit den
Ausländern seien kaum möglich. Also sprächen die Deutschen vor allem
miteinander. Ich glaube aber, daß die Türkinnen sicher mehr Deutsch
lernen würden, wenn die Deutschen mehr mit ihnen sprächen.

Dies sollte ja eigentlich ein Brief über Deutschland und Berlin werden.
Aber ich sehe schon, daß es ein Brief über mich zwischen Deutschen
und Türken wird. Na ja, das ist vielleicht auch nicht uninteressant.

Besonders interessant finde ich das türkische Familienkonzept. Meine
türkischen Kolleginnen haben z.B. oft vier, fünf oder mehr Kinder,
während die deutschen meistens nur eins oder zwei haben. Während
die deutschen Frauen ihre kleinen Kinder während des Tages in
Kindergärten schicken, sagen die Türkinnen, daß sie ihre Kinder lieber
bei Verwandten in der Türkei ließen. Sie sagen, daß das ihre Liebe° zu | *love*
ihren Kindern zeige. Sie ließen ihre Kinder lieber bei Tanten, Onkeln,
Großeltern, d.h. in der Familie zu Hause. Das wäre besser für die Kinder als
nach Deutschland zu kommen. Hier wären sie den ganzen Tag allein,
oder sie müßten bei fremden Leuten sein. Natürlich wären sie, die Mütter,
auch lieber mit ihren Kindern zusammen. Aber das ginge nun leider eben
nicht.

In der Fabrik machen die Türkinnen ihre Arbeit so gut wie die
Deutschen. Ich habe durch meine türkische Freundin Emine sehr viel
gelernt: z.B. über türkische Traditionen, die Sprache, das Essen, die
Musik. Und dann ist da die Gastfreundlichkeit° der Türken. Immer | *hospitality*
wieder sagen sie, ich solle doch zum Kaffee oder zum Abendessen
kommen. Ich habe mich bei ihnen schnell wie zu Hause gefühlt. Die
Wärme° meiner türkischen Freunde war für mich ein besonders schönes | *warmth*
Erlebnis°. | *experience*

Ich könnte noch viel von meiner deutschen (und türkischen) Welt hier erzählen. Aber es ist spät, ich bin müde, und morgen früh um sieben muß ich wieder in der Fabrik sein. Wenn Sie im Sommer wirklich nach Deutschland kommen, bitte besuchen Sie mich!

Herzliche Grüße
Sue

1. Warum wird Sues Deutsch nur langsam besser? Geben Sie zwei Gründe!

_____

_____

2. Warum hat Sue Kontakt zu deutschen und ausländischen Arbeiterinnen?

_____

_____

3. Warum ist es für manche Türkinnen schwer, Deutsch zu lernen?

_____

_____

4. Wie könnten die Deutschen ihnen helfen, mehr Deutsch zu lernen?

_____

_____

5. Welche Unterschiede gibt es zwischen deutschem und türkischem Familienkonzept?

_____

_____

6. Wer arbeitet besser, die Deutschen oder die Türkinnen?

_____

7. Was hat Sue durch ihre Freundin Emine gelernt?

_____

8. Warum hat Sue die Türkinnen besonders gern?

_____

Self-Tests

EINFÜHRUNG

A. How do you ask someone for personal information in German?
1. What is your name?
2. How old are you?
3. What is your address?
4. What is your telephone number?

B. Give the German equivalents of the following courtesy expressions.
1. thank you   2. you're welcome

C. Write out the German words for the following numbers.
1. 7   2. 12   3. 22   4. 94

D. Give the German equivalents for the following math problems.
1. $5 + 11 = 16$ 3. $6 \times 5 = 30$
2. $4 - 3 = 1$ 4. $80 \div 2 = 40$

E. 1. Give the days of the week in German.
2. Ask what day it is.
3. Say it is Thursday.

F. 1. Name five colors in German.
2. Ask what color the wall is.

G. 1. How can you tell what gender a German noun is?
2. Give the gender of the following nouns.
  a. Bleistift   d. Frau
  b. Tür   e. Mann
  c. Bett
3. Complete the sentences with the proper definite article.
  a. _____ Kugelschreiber ist neu.
  b. _____ Zimmer ist klein.
  c. _____ Lampe ist alt.
  d. Wie ist _____ Tisch? Groß oder klein?
  e. Wie alt ist _____ Uhr?
  f. _____ Kind da ist groß.

H. Complete each sentence with the pronoun that corresponds to the noun in parentheses.
1. _____ ist groß. (das Zimmer)
2. _____ ist neu. (die Adresse)
3. _____ ist zwanzig Jahre alt. (der Sekretär)
4. _____ ist zwei. (das Kind)
5. _____ ist klein. (der Stuhl)
6. _____ heißt Meyer. (die Sekretärin)

KAPITEL 1

A. 1. How would you greet someone at the following times of day?
  a. in the morning   c. in the evening
  b. in the afternoon
2. Someone asks how you are. Give one positive and one negative response.
Wie geht's?
3. A friend asks what you're doing this evening. Give three possible answers.
Was machst du heute abend?

B. 1. Give antonyms for the following words.
  a. faul   c. ernst   e. progressiv
  b. dumm d. nett   f. ruhig
2. Give two ways to say good-by in German.

C. 1. Write the German equivalent for each of the following sentences relating to time.
  a. What time is it?
  b. I'm going at one o'clock.
2. Write out the following clock times in German.
  a. 2:15   b. 3:45   c. 6:30
3. How is official time given, for example in train schedules?

D. 1. What are the three words for *you* in German?
2. Which form of *you* do you use in talking to the following people?
  a. a saleswoman   c. a friend
  b. two children   d. your mother
3. Give the German equivalents of the following English pronouns.
  a. he   c. we   e. they
  b. she d. I
4. How can you tell whether **sie** means *she* or *they?*
5. Give the German equivalents of:
  a. She plays tennis well.
  b. They play tennis well.

E. 1. What are the German equivalents of the forms of the English verb *to be?*
  a. I am   c. she is   e. you are (*3 forms*)
  b. we are d. they are

F. 1. What is the basic form of a German verb?
2. What is the most common ending of the basic verb form?
3. Give the German infinitives for the following verbs:
  a. believe b. hike   c. work

4. Give the stems of the verbs in 3 above.
5. What ending does the verb take when used
with the following subjects?
a. du   d. wir   f. sie (*sg.*)
b. ihr   e. er   g. sie (*pl.*)
c. ich
6. Complete the following sentences with the
proper form of the verb in parentheses.
a. _____ du heute Volleyball? (spielen)
b. Ich _____ gern Musik. (hören)
c. Er _____ viel. (arbeiten)
d. Gabi _____ gern. (wandern)
e. Wir _____ gern. (schwimmen)
f. Das Mädchen _____ Lore. (heißen)
g. Wie _____ du? (heißen)

G. 1. In German, one form of a verb in the present
tense is used to express ideas that require
several different forms in English. Give the
German equivalents of the following sentences.
a. You do play well.
b. Frank is working tonight.
c. Ute does work a lot.
2. The German present tense also expresses
something intended or planned for the future.
Give the German equivalents of the following
sentences.
a. I'm going to the movies this evening.
b. What will you do?

H. 1. How do you say you like to do something in
German?
2. Say that the following people like to do the
things named.
a. Ute spielt Schach.
b. Ich arbeite.
c. Wir treiben Sport.

I. 1. Where does **nicht** come in relationship to
the following:
a. predicate adjectives and nouns
b. prepositional phrases
c. specific time expressions
d. most other adverbs
e. pronouns and nouns used as objects
2. Make the following sentences negative by
adding **nicht** in the proper place.
a. Wir schwimmen gern.
b. Frank wandert viel.
c. Ich gehe ins Kino.
d. Wir arbeiten morgen.
e. Heike ist nett.
f. Ich glaube das.

J. 1. What is the first word in a specific question?
2. Where does the verb come? The subject?
3. Name three interrogative words.

4. Ask specific questions using the words in
parentheses.
a. Jürgen spielt gut Fußball. (wer)
b. Veronika spielt gern Volleyball. (was)
c. Wir gehen heute abend ins Kino. (wann)

K. 1. What is the first word in a general (yes-or-
no) question?
2. Ask whether the following statements are
really true.
a. Petra spielt oft Fußball.
b. Kurt arbeitet viel.
c. Ich spiele gut Schach.

L. 1. What word is used to form tag questions in
German?
2. Give the German equivalents of the following
sentences:
a. We're playing tennis tomorrow, aren't we?
b. Paul is tired, isn't he?
c. You like to dance, don't you? (Use **du**.)

KAPITEL 2

A. Give three types of responses to the following
statement about the weather:
Morgen ist es bestimmt schön.
1. Agree.
2. Disagree.
3. Express hope or expectation.

B. Write out the names of the months in German.

C. 1. What is the gender of the names of most
countries in German?
2. Name one feminine country and one plural
country in German.

D. Give the feminine and masculine forms of the
following nouns.
1. student   2. Swiss (citizen)   3. neighbor

E. Replace the word **heute** with **auch gestern** and
rewrite each of the following sentences in the
simple past.
1. Ich bin heute müde.
2. Eva ist heute krank.
3. Du bist heute faul.
4. Sie sind heute nervös.

F. Ask when the birthdays of the following people
are:
1. du   3. ihr
2. Frank   4. Ulrike und Kathrin

G. 1. What is a finite verb?
2. In what position is the finite verb in a German statement?

3. Rewrite the following sentences, beginning with the word in bold type.
   a. Das Wetter war **am Sonntag** nicht gut.
   b. Die Sonne scheint **hoffentlich** morgen.

H. 1. How does English generally signal the grammatical function of nouns in a sentence?
2. What type of signal does German use to indicate the grammatical function of nouns?
3. What case is used for the subject of a sentence and a predicate noun?
4. Which verbs are often followed by predicate nouns?
5. Write out the subjects and the predicate nouns in the following sentences.
   a. Gestern war das Wetter schön.
   b. Frank Schmidt ist Student.
   c. Das Mädchen heißt Cornelia.

I. 1. What is the definite article used with all plural nouns?
2. Give the plural of the following nouns, including the article.
   a. das Fenster   d. die Uhr
   b. der Tisch   e. der Stuhl
   c. das Buch   f. die Studentin

J. 1. Give the two forms of the indefinite article in German.
2. Give the English equivalents.
3. Complete the following sentences with an indefinite article.
   a. Ist das Kind _____ Mädchen oder _____ Junge?
   b. Ist die Frau _____ Nachbarin?
   c. Ist das wirklich _____ Kugelschreiber?

K. 1. What is the negative form of **ein?**
2. What are the English equivalents of the negative form of **ein?**
3. What negative do you use when the noun is preceded by a definite article?
4. Complete the following sentences with **kein or nicht,** as appropriate.
   a. Das ist _____ Uhr.
   b. Das ist _____ die Parkstraße.
   c. Warum ist _____ Stuhl hier?.

L. 1. Give the German equivalents of the following English possessive adjectives and nouns.
   a. your (*fam. sg.*) radio   d. our country
   b. their basketball   e. my address
   c. her cards
2. Give the German equivalents of the following proper names and nouns.
   a. Klaus's room   b. Tanja's watch

M. 1. Answer the following questions in the affirmative, using a personal pronoun.
   a. Ist der Tisch neu?
   b. Ist das Kind nett?
   c. Schwimmt die Frau gut?
   d. Ist die Uhr alt?
   e. Tanzen die Jungen gern?
2. Answer the following questions in the negative, using a demonstrative pronoun.
   a. Ist Dieter dumm?
   b. Ist Karin konservativ?
   c. Ist der Stuhl neu?
   d. Sind die Kinder doof?

KAPITEL 3

A. What German word do you use to contradict the assumptions in the following sentences?
1. Monika ißt keinen Fisch. _____!
2. Arbeitest du denn nicht? _____!

B. How do you say in German that you like Andrea?

C. What advice would you give to someone who said the following:
   Ich brauche etwas gegen Kopfschmerzen.

D. Give three foods/beverages a German might have at each of the following meals.
1. Frühstück 2. Mittagessen   3. Abendessen

E. 1. Which noun in a compound determines the gender?
2. Make a compound of the following nouns.
   a. der Tisch + die Lampe
   b. die Butter + das Brot

F. 1. Which forms of the verbs **essen, geben,** and **nehmen** show stem vowel change?
2. Complete the following sentences with the proper form of the verb in parentheses.
   a. Was _____ du gegen Kopfschmerzen? (nehmen)
   b. Ich _____ Aspirin. (nehmen)
   c. Zum Frühstück _____ Monika immer frische Brötchen. (essen)
   d. Wir _____ oft Eier. (essen)
   e. _____ es hier keinen Kaffee? (geben)
   f. _____ du mir zwei Mark? (geben)

G. 1. When a sentence has both time and place expressions, which comes first in English? in German?
2. Write a sentence from the following cues.
   wann / du / kommen / nach Hause / heute abend / ?

H. 1. What verb form do you use to tell someone to do something?

2. What is the position of this verb in the sentence?

3. Complete the following commands with the verb form that corresponds to the people indicated.

    a. (Monika) _____ mir bitte die Butter! (geben)

    b. (Gabi und Andrea) _____ gleich nach Hause! (kommen)

    c. (Herr Meier) _____ den Kaffee bei Messner! (kaufen)

I. 1. Which case is used for:

    a. nouns and pronouns that are subjects?

    b. nouns and pronouns that are direct objects?

2. Complete the following sentences with the possessive adjective that corresponds to the subject pronoun.

    a. Ich brauche _____ Heft wieder.

    b. Inge fragt _____ Freund Michael.

    c. Nehmt ihr _____ Bücher?

    d. Brauchst du _____ Lampe?

3. A few masculine nouns show a change in the accusative. Give the accusative form of:

    a. der Junge   b. der Nachbar

4. Name the prepositions that take accusative case.

5. Complete the following sentences, using the cues in parentheses.

    a. _____ ist von gestern. (der Kuchen)

    b. Warum kaufst du _____ ? (der Kuchen)

    c. Monika und Lars kennen _____ gut. (ihre Stadt)

    d. Uwe arbeitet für _____. (sein Professor)

    e. Habt ihr denn _____ mehr? (kein Brot)

    f. Warum kaufst du nur _____? (ein Stuhl)

    g. _____ hast du gern? (wer)

    h. Kennst du _____ da? (der Student)

    i. Gibt es hier _____ ? (kein Supermarkt)

6. Complete the following sentences with demonstrative pronouns.

    a. Der Kaffee ist gut, nicht? —Nein, _____ finde ich nicht gut.

    b. Ich brauche Brot. —Kauf _____ aber bei Meier!

    c. Wer ist der Herr da? — _____ kenne ich nicht.

7. Give the accusative forms of the following pronouns.

    a. Wie findest du _____ ? (er)

    b. Brauchst du _____ ? (ich)

    c. Wir kennen _____ nicht. (sie, *pl.*)

    d. Die Kinder haben _____ gern. (du)

e. Sie brauchen _____ heute nicht. (wir)

f. Unsere Nachbarn finden _____ lustig. (ihr)

KAPITEL 4

A. 1. Say three things in German to indicate you are preparing class work or studying.
Was machst du heute abend? —Ich

    _____.

2. Give two expressions of agreement and two expressions of regret as a response to the following request:
Willst du jetzt Kaffee trinken gehen?

B. Tell how many members of your family and relatives you have.

C. Express the following sentences in German.

1. Alex is an American.

2. He is going to be a baker.

3. Andrea is a student.

D. 1. What vowel changes do the verbs **lesen, sehen,** and **werden** have?

2. Give the irregular forms of **werden.**

3. Complete the sentences with the correct form of the verb in parentheses.

    a. Sabine _____ viel. (lesen)

    b. _____ du gern lustige Filme? (sehen)

    c. Erik _____ besser in Mathe. (werden)

E. 1. You have learned three German equivalents for *to know.* For each of the following definitions, write the appropriate German word.

    a. to know a fact

    b. to be acquainted with a person, place, or thing

    c. to know a language

2. Complete the following sentences with a form of **wissen, kennen,** or **können.**

    a. _____ du den Studenten da?

    b. Ich _____ nicht, wie er heißt.

    c. Erik _____ gut Deutsch.

    d. _____ du, wie alt Alex ist?

F. 1. What pattern of endings do the words **dieser, jeder, welcher, mancher** and **solcher** follow?

2. Which **der**-word is used only in the singular? What does it mean?

3. Which two **der**-words are used mostly in the plural? What do they mean?

4. Complete the following sentences with the correct form of the cued **der**-word.

    a. Ist _____ Café neu? (dieser)

    b. _____ Stuhl hier ist teuer. (jeder)

    c. _____ Film willst du sehen? (welcher)

d. _____ Bücher lese ich nicht. (solcher)

e. _____ Referate waren sehr gut. (mancher)

G. 1. Which kind of verb expresses an attitude about an action rather than the action itself?

2. Give the German infinitives that express the following ideas.

a. to want to   d. to be allowed to

b. to be supposed to   e. to be able to

c. to have to   f. to like

H. 1. German modals are irregular. Which forms lack endings?

2. What other irregularity do most modals show?

3. Give the proper forms of the verbs indicated.

a. ich _____ (können)

b. er _____ (dürfen)

c. du _____ (müssen)

d. wir _____ (sollen)

e. Erika _____ (wollen)

f. Ich _____ es (mögen)

I. 1. The modal **mögen** and its subjunctive form **möchte** have two different meanings. Give the German equivalents of the following sentences.

1. Do you like Inge?

2. Would you like to work this evening?

J. 1. Modal auxiliaries are generally used with dependent infinitives. Where does the infinitive come in such a sentence?

2. Rewrite the following sentences, using the modal in parentheses.

a. Arbeitest du heute? (müssen)

b. Ich verstehe alles. (können)

c. Petra sagt etwas. (wollen)

3. When is the infinitive often omitted?

4. Give the German equivalent of the following English sentence.

I have to go home now.

K. 1. Which of the following verbs are separable-prefix verbs?

a. aufhören   d. mitkommen

b. bringen   e. sehen

c. einkaufen

2. In what position is the separable prefix in the present tense and the imperative?

3. Write sentences using the guidelines.

a. Gerd / mitbringen / Bier

b. wann / du / aufstehen / morgen / ?

c. aufmachen / Fenster / ! (*use imperative, speaking to Klaus*)

d. du / wollen / mitkommen / heute abend / ?

e. ich / müssen / vorbereiten / Abendessen

KAPITEL 5

A. Name three things you would like to do during the summer vacation.

B. 1. What are the two words for *where* in German?

2. Complete the following sentences with **wo** or **wohin.**

a. Weißt du, Cornelia wohnt?

b. _____ fährst du in den Ferien?

C. Name in German three forms of private transportation and three forms of public transportation.

D. 1. What vowel change do the verbs **fahren** and **laufen** have?

2. Complete the sentences with the correct form of the verb in parentheses.

a. Wann _____ Paula nach Hamburg? (fahren)

b. Wann _____ Frank nach Hause? (laufen)

c. _____ du morgen in die Stadt? (fahren)

d. Ich _____ morgen um zehn in die Stadt. (fahren)

E. 1. When a sentence contains two time elements, which comes last, the more general or the more specific?

2. Answer the following question. **Wann stehst du morgens auf?**

F. 1. What are the five coordinating conjunctions you have learned?

2. What word means *but* in the sense of *on the contrary?*

3. What word means *but* in the sense of *nevertheless?*

4. Do coordinating conjunctions affect word order?

5. Choose the conjunction that makes sense and use it to combine the sentences.

a. Gabi bleibt zu Hause. Sie ist krank. (denn, oder)

b. Holger geht nicht schwimmen. Er spielt Tennis. (aber, sondern)

c. Er schwimmt nicht gut. Er schwimmt gern. (aber, sondern)

G. 1. Where does the verb go in a dependent clause?

2. If there are both a modal auxiliary and an infinitive, which comes last?

3. If the sentence begins with a dependent clause, does the finite verb of the independent clause come before or after the subject?

4. Combine the following sentences with the conjunction indicated.
   a. Wir können nicht fahren. (weil) Unser Auto ist kaputt.
   b. (wenn) Es regnet morgen. Wir müssen zu Hause bleiben.
5. Rewrite the following direct statements as indirect statements, using **daß.**
   a. Sabine sagt: „Sie kauft oft im Supermarkt ein."
   b. Erik glaubt: „Das Obst ist nicht so frisch."
6. Rewrite the following direct questions as indirect questions.
   a. Birgit fragt: „Kann ich direkt nach Wien fliegen?"
   b. Gerhard fragt Klaus: „Wann fährst du morgen weg?"

H. 1. What case is used in German to signal the indirect object?
2. What is the indirect object in the following sentence?
   Gerd schenkt seiner Schwester eine neue Tasche.
3. Give the dative form of the following nouns:
   a. die Beamtin   d. die Berge
   b. der Wald   e. der Student
   c. das Auto
4. Name the verbs you know that take dative.
5. Which of the following prepositions are followed by dative case?
   aus, durch, für, mit, nach, ohne, seit, von
6. Complete the following sentences with the correct form of the cued words.
   a. Der Vater erzählt _____ eine Geschichte. (die Kinder)
   b. Mit _____ gehst du in die Bibliothek? (wer)
   c. Warum glaubst du _____ nicht? (mein Bruder)
   d. Fährst du oft mit _____? (der Zug)
   e. Frank wohnt bei _____. (eine Familie)
   f. Kaufst du die Uhr für _____?(dein Vater)
   g. Erika schenkt ihrer Mutter _____. (ein Kugelschreiber)
   h. Willst du mit _____ Straßenbahn fahren? (dieser)
   i. Von _____ Nachbarn sprecht ihr? (welche)

KAPITEL 6

A. Ask a friend whether:
1. he/she is hungry.
2. he/she is thirsty.
3. the meal was good.

B. 1. Name three articles of clothing that both men and women wear.
2. Name three articles of women's clothing.

C. Form nouns by adding **-heit** or **-keit** to the following adjectives.
1. krank   2. wichtig   3. dumm

D. 1. The infinitive of a verb may be used as a noun. What gender is such a noun?
2. The English equivalent of such a noun is often a gerund. What ending does an English gerund have?
3. Give the English equivalents of the following sentences, in which one of the infinitives is used as a noun and the other as a dependent infinitive.
   a. Wandern ist gesund.
   b. Mußt du heute arbeiten?

E. 1. When is the German perfect tense used?
2. Why is it often called the "conversational past"?

F. 1. The perfect tense is a compound verb tense. What are the two parts of the verb?
2. What verb is used as the auxiliary for most verbs in the perfect tense?
3. What other verb is used as an auxiliary for some verbs in the perfect tense?
4. What conditions must be met to use the auxiliary **sein** with a past participle?
5. What two verbs are exceptions to the general rule about verbs requiring **sein?**
6. Supply the auxiliaries.
   a. Er _____ viel gearbeitet.
   b. _____ du spät aufgestanden?
   c. Wir _____ bis elf geblieben.
   d. Ilse und Paul _____ mir geholfen.
   e. _____ ihr mit dem Zug gefahren?
   f. Ich _____ gut geschlafen.

G. 1. What ending is added to the stem of a regular weak verb like **spielen** to form the past participle?
2. How is the ending different in a verb like **arbeiten,** which has a stem ending in **-t?**
3. How does an irregular weak verb like **bringen** form the participle differently from regular weak verbs?
4. Give the past participles of the following verbs.
   bringen, kosten, machen, denken, haben, kennen, regnen, wandern, wissen, tanzen

H. 1. What is the ending of the past participle of a strong verb like **sehen?**
2. What other change is characteristic for the past participle of many strong verbs?
3. Give the past participles of the following verbs.
finden, geben, helfen, lesen, nehmen, schreiben, sitzen, trinken, tun

I. 1. What happens to the **ge-**prefix in the past participle of a separable-prefix verb like **einkaufen?**
2. Give the past participles of the following verbs. anfangen, einladen, mitbringen

J. 1. How does the participle of an inseparable-prefix verb like **bekommen** differ from that of most other verbs?
2. What other type of verb adds no **ge-**prefix?
3. Give the perfect tense of the following verb phrases.
   a. Ich bestelle nichts.
   b. Wir erzählen es ihm.
   c. Verstehst du das?
   d. Sie bekommen es.
   e. Sie studiert in Bonn.
   f. Dekoriert ihr den Kuchen?

K. 1. In what position is the past participle in an independent clause?
2. Where do the past participle and the auxiliary verb come in a dependent clause?
3. Rewrite the following sentences in the perfect tense.
   a. Ich stehe spät auf, denn ich arbeite bis elf.
   b. Frank ißt viel, weil das Essen so gut schmeckt.

L. Rewrite the following sentences in the perfect tense.
1. Wen lädst du zum Essen ein?
2. Bringt ihr das Essen mit?
3. Alles sieht wirklich gut aus.
4. Jeder probiert von dem Kuchen.
5. Die Gäste bleiben bis zehn Uhr.
6. Inge kommt nicht.
7. Wir verstehen das nicht.
8. Ich schenke Gerd ein Buch, weil er mir hilft.
9. Was bekommst du zum Geburtstag?

KAPITEL 7

A. A friend asks what you do in the evening. Give three possible answers.
Was machst du abends?

B. Give two answers that express skepticism about a statement your friend makes.
Deutsche Filme sind besser als amerikanische Filme.

C. Form nouns from the following verbs by adding the suffix **-ung.** Give the English equivalents.
1. bedeuten 2. einladen 3. erzählen

D. 1. The words **hin** and **her** can be used alone or in combination with several parts of speech (for example **hierher, hinfahren**) to show direction. Which word indicates direction towards the speaker? Which indicates direction away from the speaker?
2. What position do **hin** and **her** occupy in a sentence when they stand alone?
3. Complete the following sentences with **hin, her, wo, woher,** or **wohin.**
   a. _____ wohnen Sie?
   b. _____ kommen Sie? Aus Österreich?
   c. _____ fahren Sie in den Ferien?
   d. Meine Tante wohnt in Hamburg. Ich fahre jedes Jahr _____.
   e. Kommen Sie mal _____!

E. 1. Indicate which of the following prepositions are always followed by
   a. the accusative
   b. the dative
   c. either dative or accusative
   an, auf, aus, bei, durch, für, gegen, in, nach, neben, über, von, vor, zu
2. List two contractions for each of the following prepositions:
   a. an   b. in

F. Construct sentences from the guidelines.
1. ich / fahren / in / Stadt
2. wir / gehen / auf / Markt
3. Sabine / studieren / an / Universität Hamburg
4. du / denken / an / dein / Freund /?
5. warum / Tisch / stehen / zwischen / Stühle / ?
6. Alex / arbeiten / in / ein / Buchhandlung

G. English uses *to put* and *to be* as all-purpose verbs to talk about position. German uses several different verbs. Complete the following sentences with an appropriate verb from the list.
legen, liegen, stellen, stehen, setzen, sitzen, hängen
1. Bärbel _____ die Lampe auf den Tisch.
2. Die Lampe _____ auf dem Tisch.
3. Alex _____ die Uhr an die Wand.
4. Bärbel _____ das Kind auf den Stuhl.
5. Das Kind _____ auf dem Stuhl.
6. Alex _____ das Heft auf den Tisch.
7. Das Heft _____ auf dem Tisch.
8. Er _____ das Buch in die Büchertasche.

H. 1. What case must be used for time expressions that indicate a definite time or period of time?

2. What case is used with time expressions beginning with **an, in,** or **vor?**

3. Complete the following sentences with the cued words.
   a. Wir bleiben _____. (ein / Tag)
   b. Bernd ist vor _____ weggegangen. (ein / Jahr)
   c. Susi arbeitet _____. (jeder / Abend)
   d. Er kommt in _____ wieder. (eine / Woche)

I. 1. Give the accusative and dative forms of the following pronouns.
   a. ich   c. du   e. sie (*sg.*)
   b. er   d. wir   f. Sie

2. Complete the following sentences with the proper form of the cued pronouns.
   a. Ich möchte mit _____ sprechen. (du)
   b. Was hast du _____ gefragt? (ich)
   c. Hat es _____ geschmeckt? (ihr)
   d. Kannst du _____ helfen? (sie, *pl.*)
   e. Ich habe eine Pflanze für _____ gekauft. (sie, *sg.*)
   f. Wann holst du _____ ab? (wir)
   g. Von _____ hast du gesprochen? (wer)

J. Show your understanding of the word order for direct and indirect objects by completing the sentences with the cued words.
   1. Das Hemd? Ich schenke _____ _____. (dir / es)
   2. Kaufst du _____ _____? (dieses Buch / mir)
   3. Ich gebe _____ _____ . (meinen Eltern / diese Lampe)
   4. Der Pulli? Ich schenke _____ _____ . (meinem Bruder / ihn)

K. 1. What construction is usually used in a German statement in place of a preposition + a pronoun that refers to things or ideas?
   2. What construction is used in a German question in place of a preposition + a pronoun that refers to things or ideas?
   3. When does **da-** expand to **dar-** and **wo-** expand to **wor-?**
   4. Complete the following sentences using a **da-**compound or a preposition and pronoun, as appropriate.
      a. Spricht sie oft von ihrer Reise? —Ja, sie spricht oft _____.
      b. Machst du das für deine Freundin? —Ja, ich mache das _____.
   5. Complete the sentences using a **wo-**compound or a preposition and interrogative pronoun, as appropriate.

   a. _____ spielst du morgen Tennis? —Ich spiele mit Inge.
   b. _____ habt ihr geredet? —Wir haben über den Film geredet.

KAPITEL 8

A. Name three household chores you dislike the most.

B. 1. Give two German exclamations of surprise or dismay.
   2. Give two German expressions of pleasure.

C. 1. Give opposite meanings to the following words by adding the prefix **un-.** What are the English meanings?
      a. bekannt   b. interessant.
   2. Give the English meanings of the following words.
      a. arbeitslos   b. farblos

D. Give the German words for:
   1. kitchen   3. living room
   2. first floor   4. basement

E. 1. In the genitive case, what ending is added to masculine (**der-**) and neuter (**das-**) nouns of the following kinds:
      a. one-syllable
      b. two or more syllables
      c. masculine N-nouns
   2. Give the genitive of the following nouns.
      a. das Bild   d. ein Haus
      b. dieser Laden   e. ihr Bruder
      c. der Junge
   3. What is the genitive form of **wer?**
   4. Give the German equivalent of:
      Whose stereo is that?

F. 1. Do feminine (**die-**) nouns and plural nouns add a genitive ending?
   2. Give the genitive form of the following:
      a. die Frau   c. diese Kinder
      b. eine Ausländerin d. meine Eltern

G. In German, does the genitive precede or follow the noun it modifies?

H. Name four prepositions that are followed by genitive.

I. Give the German equivalents of the following phrases.
   1. one day (indefinite time)
   2. one evening (indefinite)

© *1988 by Houghton Mifflin Company*

J. Complete the following sentences, using the cued words.
1. Wegen _____ kommt er nicht. (das Wetter)
2. Die Studenten hören die Vorlesungen _____. (der Professor)
3. Kennst du die Adresse _____ ? (mein Freund Michael)
4. Wir haben während _____ geschlafen. (die Reise)
5. Wie ist die Telefonnummer _____? (deine Freundin)
6. Kennst du die Namen _____? (die Geschäfte)

K. Complete the following sentences, using the cued words.
1. Das ist ein _____ Kind. (nett)
2. Thomas ist ein _____ Student. (gut)
3. Hans ist aber auch _____. (gut)
4. So ein _____ Geschenk habe ich noch nie bekommen. (teuer)
5. Wegen des _____ Wetters bleiben wir zu Hause. (kalt)
6. Ich esse gern Brot mit _____ Butter. (frisch)
7. Ich habe _____ Durst. (groß)
8. _____ Bier schmeckt mir nicht. (warm)
9. Die Sonne ist heute richtig _____ . (heiß)
10. Er hat seinen _____ Pulli verloren. (neu)
11. Kennen Sie die Geschichte dieser _____ Häuser? (alt)
12. Das ist keine schlechte _____. (Idee)

L. 1. How are the ordinal numbers from 2-19 formed in German?
2. Give the German words for:
   a. first   c. fifth
   b. third   d. sixteenth
3. What is added to numbers after 19 to form the ordinals?
4. Give the German words for:
   a. thirty-first   b. hundredth
5. Ordinals take adjective endings. Complete the following sentences with the cued ordinals.
   a. Am _____ November habe ich Geburtstag. (7.)
   b. Wir müssen leider ein _____ Auto kaufen. (2.)

M. 1. Ask the date in German.
2. Say it is June first.
3. Write the date, July 6, 1989, as it would appear in a letter heading.

KAPITEL 9

A. Give two expressions of regret when your friend says:
Ich kann nicht mit zur Fete. Ich fühle mich nicht wohl.

B. Name three acts of hygiene that are part of your morning ritual.

C. Complete the German expressions for:
1. *something good*   etwas _____
2. *nothing special*   nichts _____
3. *a good acquaintance*   ein guter _____
4. *a German (female)*   eine _____
5. *I have little time.*   Ich habe _____ Zeit.

D. 1. How are comparative adjectives and adverbs formed in German?
2. How do some one-syllable adjectives and adverbs change the stem vowel in the comparative?
3. Complete the following sentences using the comparative form of the cued adjective.
   a. Es ist heute _____ als gestern. (kalt)
   b. Mein neues Auto war _____ als mein altes. (teuer)
   c. Helmut wohnt jetzt in einem _____ _____ Zimmer. (groß, schön)

E. 1. How are superlative adjectives and adverbs formed in German?
2. What is the ending for the superlative if the base form ends in **-d (wild), -t (leicht),** or a sibilant **(heiß)**?
3. How do some one-syllable adjectives and adverbs change the vowel in the superlative?
4. What form does an adverb or a predicate adjective have in the superlative?
5. Complete the following sentences using the superlative form of the cued adjective or adverb.
   a. Dieser Kassettenrecorder ist _____. (teuer)
   b. Gabi arbeitet _____. (schwer)
   c. Das ist mein _____ Pulli. (schön)
   d. Gestern war der _____ Tag dieses Jahres. (kalt)

F. Give the comparative and superlative forms of:
1. gern   2. gut   3. viel

G. For each subject pronoun below, give the accusative and dative reflexive pronoun.
1. ich   3. sie *(sg. and pl.)*   5. er
2. du   4. wir

H. Some German verbs are called reflexive verbs because reflexive pronouns are regularly used with these verbs. Construct sentences using the following guidelines.
1. du / sich fühlen / heute / besser / ?
2. Cornelia / sich erkälten / gestern

I. When referring to parts of the body, German usage differs from English in some constructions. Complete the following German sentences.
1. Ich habe mir _____ Hände gewaschen.
2. Tanja putzt sich _____ Zähne.

J. 1. What word precedes the dependent infinitive with most verbs in German?
2. When are dependent infinitives *not* preceded by that word?
3. Punctuate the following sentence.
Hast du Zeit mir zu helfen?
4. What is the German construction equivalent to the English *(in order) to* + infinitive?
5. Complete the following sentences with the cued words.
   a. Es macht Spaß _____. (im Wald / wandern)
   b. Ich möchte mir _____. (eine neue Platte / kaufen)
   c. Vergiß nicht _____! (Blumen / mitbringen)
   d. Ich versuche _____. (deine Ideen / verstehen)
   e. Ich bleibe heute zu Hause _____. (um...zu / machen / meine Arbeit)

KAPITEL 10

A. Name three professions that appeal to you and three that do not.

B. Give one expression that shows you accept the following unpleasant news calmly, and give one expression of resignation:
Ich weiß, daß das Wetter furchtbar ist, aber wir müssen in die Stadt.

C. 1. When is the simple past tense used? What is it often called?
2. When is the perfect tense used? What is it often called?
3. Which verbs occur more frequently in the simple past than in the perfect tense, even in conversation?

D. 1. What is the tense marker for weak verbs in the simple past tense?
2. What is the past tense marker for **regnen, öffnen,** and verbs with stems ending in -d or -t?
3. Which forms add no endings in the simple past?
4. Change each of the following present-tense forms to simple past.
   a. ich spiele   c. es regnet
   b. Dieter arbeitet   d. wir folgen

E. 1. What tense marker is added to modals in the simple past tense?
2. What happens to modals with an umlaut in the simple past?
3. Give the simple past tense forms of the following:
   a. ich darf   c. sie muß
   b. du kannst   d. wir mögen

F. Irregular weak verbs have a vowel change in the simple past tense and several of these verbs have consonant changes. Give the simple past form of the following sentences.
1. Ich bringe den Wein.   3. Sie wissen es
2. Sie denkt an Gerd.   schon.

G. 1. How do strong verbs show the simple past tense?
2. Which forms add no endings?
3. Give the simple past tense of the following verbs.
   a. er spricht   f. ich bin
   b. sie sieht   g. sie wird
   c. ich helfe   h. sie gehen
   d. wir bleiben   i. ich fliege
   e. er fährt   j. er trägt

H. 1. Where does the prefix of separable-prefix verbs go in the simple past tense?
2. Construct sentences in the simple past, using the guidelines.
   a. Frank / einladen / uns
   b. Inge / mitbringen / Blumen
   c. ich / aufstehen / immer / früh
   d. wir / einkaufen / in / Stadt

I. 1. When is the past perfect tense used?
2. How is it formed?
3. Construct clauses in the past perfect, using the guidelines in parentheses.
   a. Ich habe gut geschlafen, (weil / ich / laufen / 20 Kilometer)
   b. Am Abend schien die Sonne, (nachdem / es / regnen / den ganzen Tag)

J. Restate the following sentences in the simple past, present perfect, and past perfect tenses.

1. Stefan schreibt den Brief.
2. Inge geht nach Hause.

K. Als, **wenn,** and **wann** are equivalent to English *when.*
1. Which must be used for *when* to introduce direct or indirect questions?
2. Which must be used for *when* in the sense of *whenever* (that is, for repeated events or habitual actions), regardless of time?
3. Which must be used for *when* in clauses with events in the present or future?
4. Which must be used for *when* in clauses concerned with a single past event?
5. Complete the following sentences with **als, wenn,** or **wann,** as appropriate.
   a. Wir haben viel Spaß, _____ Schmidts uns besuchen.
   b. Sie kamen mit, _____ wir gestern ins Café gingen.
   c. Immer, _____ wir schwimmen wollten regnete es.
   d. Ich weiß nicht, _____ wir zurückgekommen sind.

KAPITEL 11

A. Name three hobbies you have or would like to have.

B. Name three things you would like to do during the summer.

C. 1. What construction do you use to indicate a continuing increase in the quantity, quality, or degree expressed by an adjective or adverb?
2. Complete the following sentences using the construction you described above.
   a. *Mrs. Fischer is working more and more.*
      Frau Fischer arbeitet _____.
   b. *The problems are getting bigger and bigger.*
      Die Probleme werden _____.

D. Form diminutives from the following nouns.
   1. Haus   2. Buch   3. Hand   4. Schlaf

E. Give two favorable answers and a negative answer to your friend's question. Use **würde**-constructions and/or the subjunctive.
   Hättest du Lust, nach Deutschland zu fliegen?

F. 1. Give three uses of the **würde**-construction and the subjunctive.
2. Say that Trudi would also like to do the following. Use **würde.**
   Christoph faulenzt viel.

3. Say that you wish the following situation were different. Use **würde.**
   Die Sonne scheint nicht.
4. Restate as a request, using **würde.**
   Bleib noch eine Stunde!

G. 1. How is the present-time subjunctive of strong verbs formed?
2. Give the subjunctive of the following verb forms.
   a. er ist   c. sie fahren
   b. sie fliegt   d. du bleibst

H. 1. How is the present-time subjunctive of weak verbs formed?
2. Give the subjunctive of the following verb forms.
   a. sie lernt   b. du arbeitest

I. 1. How is the present-time subjunctive of irregular weak verbs formed?
2. Give the subjunctive of the following verb forms.
   a. sie bringt   c. wir haben
   b. ich denke

J. 1. How is the present-time subjunctive of modals formed?
2. Give the subjunctive of the following verb forms.
   a. ich muß   b. du kannst

K. 1. How is the past-time subjunctive formed?
2. Give the past-time subjunctive of the following verb forms.
   a. wir sind   c. ich mache mit
   b. er singt

L. 1. When a modal is used in the past-time subjunctive with a dependent infinitive, what form does the past participle of the modal have?
2. Restate in the past-time subjunctive:
   Ich könnte das allein machen.

M. 1. What are the two clauses in a conditional sentence called?
2. What word begins the condition clause?
3. In what kind of conditional sentence is the indicative used?
4. In what kind of conditional sentence are the **würde**-construction and the subjunctive used?
5. Restate as conditions contrary to fact, both in the present time and in the past time.
   a. Christine fliegt nach Dänemark, wenn sie Zeit hat.
   b. Wenn ich Geld habe, esse ich im Restaurant.

N. Construct sentences using the guidelines.
1. ich / tun / das / nicht (*present-time subj.*)
2. du / glauben / mir / nicht (*use* **würde**)
3. wir / können / fahren / morgen (*present-time subj.*)
4. Wenn sie Geld hätte, sie / kaufen / ein neues Auto (*use* **würde**)
5. Ich hätte das getan, wenn / ich / wissen / das (*past-time subj.*)
6. Ich wollte, du / können / bleiben / länger (*present-time subj.*)

KAPITEL 12

A. Give two responses that show you're not entirely sure of your answer.
Bist du am Samstag nachmittag frei?

B. Give the following fractions in German.
1. 1/2   2. 3/4   3. 1/3

C. Form adjectives or adverbs from the following nouns by adding **-lich.** Give the English equivalents.
1. Frage   2. Tag

D. 1. How is the future tense formed in German?
2. In an independent clause where the future is used, what position is the infinitive in?
3. In a dependent clause where the future is used, what verb forms are in the final position?
4. Restate in the future tense.
   a. Inge hilft uns.
   b. Machst du das wirklich?
   c. Michael sagt, daß er einen neuen Job sucht. (*Do not change* **Michael sagt.**)

E. 1. What form do modals have in the future tense?
2. What position do the modals occupy?
3. Restate in the future tense.
   a. Silke muß ihre Arbeit allein machen.
   b. Kannst du bestimmt kommen?

F. 1. When is the present tense used to express future time?
2. Name three uses of the future tense.
3. Construct sentences using the guidelines.
   a. ich / anrufen / dich / heute abend (*present tense to express future*)
   b. wir / essen / wohl / um sieben (*present probability*)
   c. ich / helfen / meinen Freunden (*determination*)

G. Show your understanding of the various meanings of **lassen** by giving the English equivalents of the following sentences.
1. Laß mich heute abwaschen!
2. Wo hast du wieder deine Handschuhe gelassen?
3. Ich muß leider meinen Kassettenrecorder reparieren lassen.
4. Laßt uns gehen!

H. 1. In the future tense in what position is **lassen** when it is used with a dependent infinitive?
2. Restate in the future tense.
   Ich lasse es Sie morgen wissen.

I. 1. What two forms does the past participle of **lassen** have?
2. Which form is used when **lassen** has a dependent infinitive?
3. Restate the following sentences in the perfect tense.
   a. Warum läßt du Kurt dein Auto fahren?
   b. Ich lasse meine Schlüssel zu Hause.

J. 1. What function does a relative pronoun serve?
2. Where do the verb and auxiliary come in a relative clause?

K. 1. With what forms are most of the relative pronoun forms identical?
2. The following pronoun forms are exceptions. Give the relative pronouns for:
   a. dative plural
   b. genitive masculine and neuter
   c. genitive feminine singular and plural

L. 1. How do you decide the gender and number of the relative pronoun you use?
2. How do you decide what case of a relative pronoun to use?
3. What case does a relative pronoun have when it follows a preposition?

M. Complete the following sentences with a relative pronoun.
1. Ist das der Mann, _____ soviel arbeitet?
2. Wie heißt die Frau, von _____ du gerade erzählt hast?
3. Was hältst du von Eltern, _____ Kinder laut sind?
4. Wo ist das Restaurant, in _____ wir morgen essen?
5. Wie gefällt dir der Pulli, _____ du zum Geburtstag bekommen hast?
6. Die Freunde, mit _____ wir in den Ferien waren, sind wirklich nette Leute.

7. Ich arbeite für einen Chef, _____ nichts paßt!

8. Frank arbeitet für eine Chefin, _____ fließend Englisch kann.

9. Mit dem wenigen Geld, _____ ich diese Woche verdient habe, kann ich nicht viel anfangen.

KAPITEL 13

A. A friend assumes you're going along to a concert. Give two enthusiastic replies and two less enthusiastic ones.
Du gehst doch mit ins Konzert, nicht?

B. 1. What is the role of the subject of a sentence in active voice?
2. What is the role of the subject in passive voice?

C. 1. How is passive voice formed in German?
2. In the perfect tense of the passive voice what participle is used in place of **geworden?**
3. Complete the following sentence.
Die Arbeit ist gemacht _____.
4. Construct sentences using the guidelines.
a. Essen / kochen / gerade (*passive, simple past*)
b. Badezimmer / putzen / jeden Tag (*passive, simple past*)
c. Bett / machen (*passive, future*)
d. Brief / schreiben / heute noch (*passive, present*)
e. Autos / reparieren / hier (*passive, present*)

D. 1. In English the agent in the passive voice is the object of the preposition *by: The work was done by our neighbors.* How is the agent expressed in German?
2. How is "means" expressed in passive in German?
3. Complete the following sentences.
a. Die Nachbarn wurden _____ die laute Musik gestört.
b. Die Arbeit wurde _____ unseren Nachbarn gemacht.

E. 1. Modals may be used with a passive infinitive. How is a passive infinitive formed?
2. Complete the following sentences with the passive infinitive of the cued verbs.
a. Wann muß die Arbeit _____? (machen)
b. Der Geschirrspüler kann nicht mehr _____ . (reparieren)

F. 1. What case do dative objects in active voice have in passive voice?
2. Give the English equivalents.
a. Mir wurde nicht geglaubt.

b. Ihm wird geholfen.

G. 1. In an impersonal passive, what happens to the dummy subject **es** if some other word begins the sentence?
2. Begin the following sentence with **es.**
Bis spät in die Nacht wurde getanzt.
3. Begin the following sentence with **hier.**
Es wird hier nur deutsch gesprochen.

H. 1. How does the past participle function in the construction **sein** + participle?
2. What is the **sein** + participle construction often called?
3. Complete the German sentences so that their meanings are equivalent to the English.
a. The problem is being solved.
Das Problem _____ gelöst.
b. The clothes are washed.
Die Wäsche _____ gewaschen.
c. Mark is invited.
Mark _____ eingeladen.
d. The stereo is being repaired.
Die Stereoanlage _____ repariert.

I. 1. What are three uses of **werden?**
2. Identify the use of **werden** and give the English equivalents for the following sentences.
a. Eine Reise in die DDR wurde geplant.
b. Es wird endlich wärmer.
c. Er wird an uns schreiben.

J. 1. Give four substitutes for the passive voice.
2. Restate the following sentences, substituting the construction in parentheses for the passive.
a. Das darf nicht vergessen werden. (man)
b. Wie kann man das erklären? (sein + zu)
c. In Deutschland sind natürliche Sachen leichter zu verkaufen. (*reflexive construction*)
d. Mit der Chefin kann man gut reden. (sich lassen)
e. Da kann man nichts machen. (sein + zu)
f. Die Platte muß bestellt werden. (man)
g. Eine Programmiersprache kann nicht so leicht gelernt werden. (sein + zu)
h. Blumenläden sind überall zu finden. (*reflexive construction*)
i. Man kann das Auto leicht reparieren. (sich lassen)

KAPITEL 14

A. Name three subjects that interest you in the newspaper.
Was interessiert Sie in der Zeitung?

B. 1. What verb forms are often used for indirect discourse in German?

2. Complete the following sentences with the appropriate general subjunctive form of the cued verb.

   a. Christiane hat gesagt, daß sie keine Zeit _____. (haben, *present time*)

   b. Uwe hat gesagt, daß er mit seinem Chef _____. (sprechen, *past time*)

   c. Ursel hat gesagt, daß du uns _____. (helfen, *future time*)

   d. Martin hat gesagt, daß er Schreibmaschine schreiben _____. (können, *present time*)

C. 1. How do you determine whether to use present-, past-, or future-time subjunctive in indirect discourse?

   2. Change the sentences from direct discourse to indirect discourse, using general subjunctive.

   a. Christoph hat gesagt: „Ich bin unschuldig.“

   b. Gabi hat gesagt: „Ich habe eine neue Stelle gefunden.“

   c. Holger hat gesagt: „Ich werde nicht streiken.“

D. Rewrite the following direct questions as indirect questions, using general subjunctive.

   1. Beate hat gefragt: „Kommen Jürgen und Dirk mit?“

   2. Dirk hat gefragt: „Wie lange sind sie geblieben?“

   3. Erika hat gefragt: „War der Urlaub schön?“

E. 1. How do you form indirect commands in German?

   2. Form indirect commands using the guidelines. Use general subjunctive.

   a. Ingrid hat mir gesagt, (ich / treffen / sie / um vier)

   b. Richard hat Christel gesagt, (sie / mitbringen / Cola)

   c. Tanja hat uns gesagt, (wir / mitkommen)

F. 1. What is the difference in meaning between special and general subjunctive?

   2. When is special subjunctive used?

   3. What person of special subjunctive verbs is most commonly used?

G. 1. How is present-time special subjunctive formed?

   2. Give both the special and general subjunctive forms of the following verbs.

   a. sie fährt   d. er hat

   b. er spricht   e. sie kann

   c. sie wird   f. er muß

H. Give the special and general subjunctive forms of **sein**.

   1. ich   3. Inge

   2. du   4. wir

I. 1. How is past-time special subjunctive formed?

   2. Give the past-time forms of both special and general subjunctive.

   a. sie findet   c. sie arbeitet

   b. er läuft   d. er geht

J. Complete the sentences in indirect discourse by using the cued verbs in special subjunctive.

   1. Beate hat gesagt, daß sie klassische Musik schön _____. (finden, *present time*)

   2. Dirk hat gesagt, daß er das nicht verstehen _____. (können, *present time*)

   3. Bärbel hat gefragt, was Cornelia im Urlaub _____. (machen, *past time*)

   4. Uwe hat gefragt, ob Cornelia mit dem Zug _____. (fahren, *past time*)

Answer Key to Self-Tests

SELF-TEST ANSWERS: EINFÜHRUNG

A. 1. Wie heißen Sie?
2. Wie alt sind Sie?
3. Wie ist Ihre Adresse?
4. Wie ist Ihre Telefonnummer?

B. 1. danke   2. bitte

C. 1. sieben   3. zweiundzwanzig
2. zwölf   4. vierundneunzig

D. 1. Fünf und elf ist sechzehn.
2. Vier weniger drei ist eins.
3. Sechs mal fünf ist dreißig.
4. Achtzig (dividiert) durch zwei ist vierzig.

E. 1. Montag, Dienstag, Mittwoch, Donnerstag, Freitag, Samstag (Sonnabend), Sonntag
2. Welcher Tag ist heute?
3. Heute ist Donnerstag.

F. 1. blau, braun, gelb, grau, grün, rot, schwarz, weiß
2. Welche Farbe hat die Wand?

G. 1. By the article and the pronoun that refer to the noun.
2. a. masculine, der Bleistift
b. feminine, die Tür
c. neuter, das Bett
d. feminine, die Frau
e. masculine, der Mann
3. a. der Kugelschreiber   d. der Tisch
b. das Zimmer   e. die Uhr
c. die Lampe   f. das Kind

H. 1. Es   3. Er   5. Er
2. Sie   4. Es   6. Sie

SELF-TEST ANSWERS: KAPITEL 1

A. 1. a. Guten Morgen!
b. Guten Tag!
c. Guten Abend!
2. Answers will vary. Possibilities are:
Positive: Gut, danke. / Danke, ganz gut.
Negative: Nicht so gut. / (Mir geht's) schlecht.
3. Answers will vary.

B. 1. a. fleißig   d. doof
b. intelligent   e. konservativ
c. lustig   f. nervös

2. Auf Wiedersehen; Tschüß

C. 1. a. Wieviel Uhr (Wie spät) ist es?
b. Ich gehe um ein Uhr.
2. a. Viertel nach zwei
b. Viertel vor vier
c. halb sieben
3. Official time uses a 24-hour clock.

D. 1. du, ihr, Sie
2. a. Sie   b. ihr   c. du   d. du
3. a. er   c. wir   e. sie
b. sie   d. ich
4. By the verb: sie + singular verb = *she;*
sie + plural verb = *they*
5. a. Sie spielt gut Tennis.
b. Sie spielen gut Tennis.

E. 1. a. ich bin   d. sie sind
b. wir sind   e. du bist; ihr seid; Sie sind
c. sie ist

F. 1. the infinitive   2. -en
3. a. glauben   b. wandern   c. arbeiten
4. a. glaub-   b. wander-   c. arbeit-
5. a. -st   d. -en   f. -t
b. -t   e. -t   g. -en
c. -e
6. a. Spielst   e. schwimmen
b. höre   f. heißt
c. arbeitet   g. heißt
d. wandert

G. 1. a. Du spielst gut.
b. Frank arbeitet heute abend.
c. Ute arbeitet viel.
2. a. Ich gehe heute abend ins Kino.
b. Was machst du? (macht ihr, machen Sie?)

H. 1. Use **gern** + verb.
2. a. Ute spielt gern Schach.
b. Ich arbeite gern.
c. Wir treiben gern Sport.

I. 1. a. before predicate adjectives and nouns.
b. before prepositional phrases
c. after specific time expressions
d. before most other adverbs
e. after pronouns and nouns used as objects
2. a. Wir schwimmen nicht gern.
b. Frank wandert nicht viel.

c. Ich gehe nicht ins Kino.
d. Wir arbeiten morgen nicht.
e. Heike ist nicht nett.
f. Ich glaube das nicht.

J. 1. the interrogative expression
2. The verb comes second, after the interrogative. The subject comes after the verb.
3. wann, was, wer, wie, wieviel
4. a. Wer spielt gut Fußball?
   b. Was spielt Veronika gern?
   c. Wann gehen wir ins Kino?

K. 1. the verb
2. a. Spielt Petra wirklich oft Fußball?
   b. Arbeitet Kurt wirklich viel?
   c. Spielst du wirklich gut Schach?

L. 1. nicht
2. a. Wir spielen morgen Tennis, nicht?
   b. Paul ist müde, nicht?
   c. Du tanzt gern, nicht?

SELF-TEST ANSWERS: KAPITEL 2

A. Answers will vary. Possible ones are:
1. Ja, morgen ist es bestimmt schön.
2. Ich glaube nicht.
3. Hoffentlich. / Ja, vielleicht.

B. Januar, Februar, März, April, Mai, Juni, Juli, August, September, Oktober, November, Dezember

C. 1. neuter (das)　　2. die Schweiz; die USA

D. 1. die Studentin; der Student
2. die Schweizerin; der Schweizer
3. die Nachbarin; der Nachbar

E. 1. Ich war auch gestern müde.
2. Eva war auch gestern krank.
3. Du warst auch gestern faul.
4. Sie waren auch gestern nervös.

F. 1. Wann hast du Geburtstag?
2. Wann hat Frank Geburtstag?
3. Wann habt ihr Geburtstag?
4. Wann haben Ulrike und Kathrin Geburtstag?

G. 1. A finite verb is the principal verb of a sentence or clause. It agrees with the subject.
2. second
3. a. Am Sonntag war das Wetter nicht gut.
   b. Hoffentlich scheint die Sonne morgen.

H. 1. by word order　　3. the nominative case
2. case　　4. sein; heißen
5. a. subject = das Wetter
   b. subject = Frank Schmidt; pred. noun = Student
   c. subject = das Mädchen; pred. noun = Cornelia

I. 1. die
2. a. die Fenster　　d. die Uhren
   b. die Tische　　e. die Stühle
   c. die Bücher　　f. die Studentinnen

J. 1. ein; eine
2. a, an
3. a. ein Mädchen; ein Junge
   b. eine Nachbarin
   c. ein Kugelschreiber

K. 1. kein　　2. not a; not any; no　　3. nicht
4. a. keine　　b. nicht　　c. kein

L. 1. a. dein Radio　　d. unser Land
   b. ihr Basketball　　e. meine Adresse
   c. ihre Karten
2. a. Klaus' Zimmer　　b. Tanjas Uhr

M. 1. a. Ja, er ist neu.
   b. Ja, es ist nett.
   c. Ja, sie schwimmt gut.
   d. Ja, sie ist alt.
   e. Ja, sie tanzen gern.
2. a. Nein, der ist nicht dumm.
   b. Nein, die ist nicht konservativ.
   c. Nein, der ist nicht neu.
   d. Nein, die sind nicht doof.

SELF-TEST ANSWERS: KAPITEL 3

A. 1. Doch!　　2. Doch!

B. Ich habe Andrea gern.

C. Answers will vary: Nimm doch Aspirin! / Geh doch in die Apotheke!

D. Answers may vary.
1. Frühstück: Brötchen, Butter, Eier, Kaffee
2. Mittagessen: Fisch, Gemüse, Fleisch, Kartoffeln, Obst
3. Abendessen: Käse, Brot, Wurst, Bier, Mineralwasser, Tee

E. 1. the last noun
2. a. die Tischlampe　　b. das Butterbrot

F. 1. second (**du**) and third (**er/es/sie**) person singular

2. a. nimmst   d. essen
   b. nehme   e. Gibt
   c. ißt   f. Gibst

G. 1. Time follows place in English. Time precedes place in German.
2. Wann kommst du heute abend nach Hause?

H. 1. the imperative
2. first position
3. a. Gib   b. Kommt   c. Kaufen Sie

I. 1. a. nominative case   b. accusative case
2. a. mein   c. eure
   b. ihren   d. deine
3. a. den Jungen   b. den Nachbarn
4. durch, für, gegen, ohne, um
5. a. Der Kuchen   e. kein Brot
   b. den Kuchen   f. einen Stuhl
   c. ihre Stadt   g. Wen
   d. seinen Professor   h. den Studenten
                  i. keinen Supermarkt
6. a. den   b. das   c. Den
7. a. ihn   c. sie   e. uns
   b. mich   d. dich   f. euch

SELF-TEST ANSWERS: KAPITEL 4

A. Answers will vary. Some possible ones are:
1. Ich bereite mein Referat vor. / Ich schreibe meine Seminararbeit. / Ich lerne für die Klausur. / Ich lese einen Artikel über...
2. Agreement: Ja, gern. / Klar. / Natürlich. Regret: Ich kann leider nicht. / Tut mir leid. / Ich habe kein Geld.

B. Answers will vary. Ich habe einen Bruder, eine Schwester, vier Tanten, usw.

C. 1. Alex ist Amerikaner.
2. Er wird Bäcker.
3. Andrea ist Studentin.

D. 1. **lesen** and **sehen** change e to ie; **werden** changes e to i
2. du wirst, er/sie wird
3. a. liest   b. Siehst   c. wird

E. 1. a. wissen   b. kennen   c. können
2. a. Kennst   c. kann
   b. weiß   d. Weißt

F. 1. the same as the definite articles
2. **jeder**; it means *each, every*

3. **manche, solche; manche** means *some*, **solche** means *such*
4. a. dieses Café   d. Solche Bücher
   b. Jeder Stuhl   e. Manche Referate
   c. Welchen Film

G. 1. modal auxiliary
2. a. wollen   d. dürfen
   b. sollen   e. können
   c. müssen   f. mögen

H. 1. first, (ich) and third (er/es/sie) person singular
2. a stem-vowel change
3. a. ich kann   d. wir sollen
   b. er darf   e. Erika will
   c. du mußt   f. Ich mag es

I. 1. Magst du Inge? / Mögen Sie Inge?
2. Möchtest du heute abend arbeiten? / Möchten Sie heute abend arbeiten?

J. 1. in last position
2. a. Mußt du heute arbeiten?
   b. Ich kann alles verstehen.
   c. Petra will etwas sagen.
3. When the meaning of the infinitive is clear from the sentence.
4. Ich muß jetzt nach Hause.

K. 1. The separable-prefix verbs are **aufhören, einkaufen, mitkommen.**
2. in last position
3. a. Gerd bringt Bier mit.
   b. Wann stehst du morgen auf?
   c. Mach das Fenster auf!
   d. Willst du heute abend mitkommen?
   e. Ich muß das Abendessen vorbereiten.

SELF-TEST ANSWERS: KAPITEL 5

A. Answers will vary: Ich möchte wandern, viel schwimmen, Tennis spielen, schlafen, usw.

B. 1. wo; wohin
2. a. wo   b. Wohin

C. Private: das Auto, das Fahrrad, das Flugzeug, das Mofa, das Motorrad
Public: der Bus, das Flugzeug, die Straßenbahn, die U-Bahn, das Schiff, der Zug

D. 1. **a** to **ä** in second (**du**) and third (**er/es/sie**) persons
2. a. fährt   c. Fährst
   b. läuft   d. fahre

E. 1. The more specific element comes last.
   2. Ich stehe morgens um (sieben) auf.

F. 1. aber, denn, oder, sondern, und
   2. sondern   3. aber   4. no
   5. a. Gabi bleibt zu Hause, denn sie ist
         krank.
      b. Holger geht nicht schwimmen, sondern
         er spielt Tennis.
      c. Er schwimmt nicht gut, aber er
         schwimmt gern.

G. 1. in last position
   2. modal auxiliary comes last
   3. The finite verb comes before the subject.
   4. a. Wir können nicht fahren, weil unser
         Auto kaputt ist.
      b. Wenn es morgen regnet, müssen wir zu
         Hause bleiben.
   5. a. Sabine sagt, daß sie oft im Supermarkt
         einkauft.
      b. Erik glaubt, daß das Obst nicht so frisch
         ist.
   6. a. Birgit fragt, ob sie direkt nach Wien
         fliegen kann.
      b. Gerhard fragt Klaus, wann er morgen
         wegfährt.

H. 1. dative
   2. seiner Schwester
   3. a. der Beamtin   d. den Bergen
      b. dem Wald   e. dem Studenten
      c. dem Auto
   4. danken, gehören, glauben
   5. aus, mit, nach, seit, von
   6. a. den Kindern   f. deinen Vater
      b. wem   g. einen
      c. meinem Bruder   Kugelschreiber
      d. dem Zug   h. dieser Straßenbahn
      e. einer Familie   i. welchen

SELF-TEST ANSWERS: KAPITEL 6

A. 1. Hast du Hunger?
   2. Hast du Durst?
   3. Hat es geschmeckt? / War das Essen gut?

B. 1. der Handschuh, der Pulli, der Regenman-
      tel, der Schuh, der Hut, das Hemd, die
      Hose, die Jacke, die Socken, die Jeans
   2. der Rock, der Strumpf, das Kleid, die
      Bluse

C. 1. die Krankheit
   2. die Wichtigkeit
   3. die Dummheit

D. 1. neuter
   2. -ing
   3. a. Hiking is healthy.
      b. Do you have to work today?

E. 1. To refer to past actions or states.
   2. It is used especially in conversation.

F. 1. the past participle of the verb and an
      auxiliary
   2. haben
   3. sein
   4. The verb must (1) be intransitive and (2)
      indicate change of condition or location or
      position.
   5. bleiben; sein
   6. a. hat   d. haben
      b. Bist   e. Seid
      c. sind   f. habe

G. 1. -t   2. adds -et instead of -t
   3. There is a vowel change and sometimes
      a consonant change: gebracht
   4. gebracht, gekostet, gemacht, gedacht,
      gehabt, gekannt, geregnet, gewandert,
      gewußt, getanzt

H. 1. -n or -en
   2. Some participles have a vowel change; a
      few also have consonant changes.
   3. gefunden, gegeben, geholfen, gelesen,
      genommen, geschrieben, gesessen,
      getrunken, getan

I. 1. The prefix ge- comes between the prefix
      and the stem of the participle: eingekauft.
   2. angefangen, eingeladen, mitgebracht

J. 1. It adds no ge-prefix.
   2. verbs ending in -ieren
   3. a. Ich habe nichts bestellt.
      b. Wir haben es ihm erzählt.
      c. Hast du das verstanden?
      d. Sie haben es bekommen.
      e. Sie hat in Bonn studiert.
      f. Habt ihr den Kuchen dekoriert?

K. 1. in final position
   2. The auxiliary follows the past participle
      and is in final position.
   3. a. Ich bin spät aufgestanden, denn ich habe
         bis elf gearbeitet.
      b. Frank hat viel gegessen, weil das Essen
         so gut geschmeckt hat.

L. 1. Wen hast du zum Essen eingeladen?
2. Habt ihr das Essen mitgebracht?
3. Alles hat wirklich gut ausgesehen.
4. Jeder hat von dem Kuchen probiert.
5. Die Gäste sind bis zehn Uhr geblieben.
6. Inge ist nicht gekommen.
7. Wir haben das nicht verstanden.
8. Ich habe Gerd ein Buch geschenkt, weil er mir geholfen hat.
9. Was hast du zum Geburtstag bekommen?

SELF-TEST ANSWERS: KAPITEL 7

A. Answers will vary. Possible ones are: Ich sehe fern. / Ich treffe Freunde in der Kneipe. / Ich lese. / Ich arbeite.

B. Answers will vary. Possible ones are: Wirklich? / Meinst du? / Was hast du gegen amerikanische Filme? / Ich sehe das ganz anders.

C. 1. die Bedeutung = the meaning
2. die Einladung = the invitation
3. die Erzählung = the story, account, narrative

D. 1. **Her** indicates direction towards the speaker; **hin** indicates direction away from the speaker.
2. last position
3. a. Wo   d. hin
   b. Woher   e. her
   c. Wohin

E. 1. a. accusative: durch, für, gegen
   b. dative: aus, bei, nach, von, zu
   c. either-or: an, auf, in, neben, über, vor
2. a. ans, am   b. ins, im

F. 1. Ich fahre in die Stadt.
2. Wir gehen auf den Markt.
3. Sabine studiert an der Universität Hamburg.
4. Denkst du an deinen Freund?
5. Warum steht der Tisch zwischen den Stühlen?
6. Alex arbeitet in einer Buchhandlung.

G. 1. stellt   4. setzt   7. liegt
2. steht   5. sitzt   8. steckt
3. hängt   6. legt

H. 1. accusative   2. dative
3. a. einen Tag   c. jeden Abend
   b. einem Jahr   d. einer Woche

I. 1.

	acc.	*dat.*
a. ich	mich	mir
b. er	ihn	ihm
c. du	dich	dir
d. wir	uns	uns
e. sie	sie	ihr
f. Sie	Sie	Ihnen

2. a. dir   d. ihnen   f. uns
   b. mich   e. sie   g. wem
   c. euch

J. 1. es dir   2. mir dieses Buch
3. meinen Eltern diese Lampe
4. ihn meinem Bruder

K. 1. **da**-compound   2. **wo**-compound
3. When the preposition begins with a vowel.
4. a. davon   b. für sie
5. a. Mit wem   b. Worüber

SELF-TEST ANSWERS: KAPITEL 8

A. Answers will vary. Possible answers: abwaschen, abtrocknen, Küche sauber machen, (Schlafzimmer, Garage, usw.) aufräumen, kochen

B. Answers will vary. Possible ones are:
1. ach / merkwürdig / O je
2. ah gut / ausgezeichnet / Das macht Spaß. / phantastisch / schön / toll

C. 1. a. unbekannt = unknown
   b. uninteressant = uninteresting
2. a. without work, unemployed
   b. colorless

D. 1. die Küche   3. das Wohnzimmer
2. das Erdgeschoß   4. der Keller

E. 1. a. -es   b. -s   c. -(e)n
2. a. des Bildes   d. eines Hauses
   b. dieses Ladens   e. ihres Bruders
   c. des Jungen
3. wessen
4. Wessen Stereoanlage ist das?

F. 1. no
2. a. der Frau   c. dieser Kinder
   b. einer Ausländerin   d. meiner Eltern

G. The genitive follows the noun it modifies.

H. (an)statt, trotz, während, wegen

I. a. eines Tages   b. eines Abends

J. 1. des Wetters   4. der Reise
    2. des Professors   5. deiner Freundin
    3. meines Freundes   6. der Geschäfte
      Michael

K. 1. nettes   5. kalten   9. heiß
    2. guter   6. frischer   10. neuen
    3. gut   7. großen   11. alten
    4. teures   8. Warmes   12. schlechte

L. 1. By adding **-t** to the numbers.
    2. a. erst-   c. fünft-
      b. dritt-   d. sechzehnt-
    3. **-st** is added.
    4. a. einunddreißigst-   b. hundertst-
    5. a. siebten   b. zweites

M. 1. Den wievielten haben wir heute?
    2. Heute haben wir den ersten Juni.
    3. den 6. Juli 1989 / 6.7.89

SELF-TEST ANSWERS: KAPITEL 9

A. Answers will vary. Possible ones are: Das ist Pech. / Ach, wie dumm. / Das tut mir leid. / Hoffentlich fühlst du dich morgen besser. / Schade.

B. Possible answers: Ich dusche mich. / Ich putze mir die Zähne. / Ich rasiere mich. / Ich kämme mich. / Ich wasche mir Gesicht und Hände.

C. 1. etwas Gutes   4. eine Deutsche
    2. nichts Besonderes   5. wenig Zeit
    3. ein guter Bekannter

D. 1. **-er** is added to the base form.
    2. The vowel a, o, or u adds umlaut.
    3. a. kälter   b. teurer   c. größeren, schöneren

E. 1. **-st** is added to the base form   2. **-est**
    3. The vowel a, o, or u adds umlaut.
    4. am + (e)sten
    5. a. am teuersten   c. schönster
      b. am schwersten   d. kälteste

F. 1. lieber, am liebsten
    2. besser, am besten
    3. mehr, am meisten

G. 1. mich, mir   4. uns, uns
    2. dich, dir   5. sich, sich
    3. sich, sich

H. 1. Fühlst du dich heute besser?
    2. Cornelia hat sich gestern erkältet.

I. 1. die Hände   2. die Zähne

J. 1. zu   2. when used with modals
    3. Hast du Zeit, mir zu helfen?
    4. **um...zu** + infinitive
    5. a. Es macht Spaß, *im Wald zu wandern.*
      b. Ich möchte mir *eine neue Platte kaufen.*
      c. Vergiß nicht, *Blumen mitzubringen!*
      d. Ich versuche, *deine Ideen zu verstehen.*
      e. Ich bleibe heute zu Hause, *um meine Arbeit zu machen.*

SELF-TEST ANSWERS: KAPITEL 10

A. Answers will vary.

B. Answers will vary. Possible ones are: Das habe ich mir schon gedacht. / Das macht nichts. / Na, wenn schon. / Da kann man nichts machen. / Wenn es sein muß.

C. 1. to narrate a series of connected events in the past; often called narrative past.
    2. in a two-way exchange to talk about events in the past; often called conversational past
    3. modals, **sein, haben**

D. 1. -te   2. -ete
    3. first (**ich**) and third (**er/es/sie**) persons
    4. a. ich spielte   c. es regnete
      b. Dieter arbeitete   d. wir folgten

E. 1. -te   2. They lose the umlaut.
    3. a. ich durfte   c. sie mußte
      b. du konntest   d. wir mochten

F. 1. Ich brachte den Wein.
    2. Sie dachte an Gerd.
    3. Sie wußten es schon.

G. 1. They undergo a stem change.
    2. first (**ich**) and third (**er/es/sie**) persons
    3. a. er sprach   e. er fuhr   h. sie gingen
      b. sie sah   f. ich war   i. ich flog
      c. ich half   g. sie wurde   j. er trug
      d. wir blieben

H. 1. in final position
    2. a. Frank lud uns ein.
      b. Inge brachte Blumen mit.
      c. Ich stand immer früh auf.
      d. Wir kauften in der Stadt ein.

I. 1. It is used to report an event or action that took place before another event or action in the past.

2. It consists of the simple past of the auxiliaries **haben** or **sein** and the past participle of the verb.
3. a. ... weil ich 20 Kilometer gelaufen war.
   b. ... nachdem es den ganzen Tag geregnet hatte.

J. 1. Stefan schrieb den Brief. Stefan hat den Brief geschrieben. Stefan hatte den Brief geschrieben.
2. Inge ging nach Hause. Inge ist nach Hause gegangen. Inge war nach Hause gegangen.

K. 1. wann   2. wenn   3. wenn   4. als
5. a. wenn   b. als   c. wenn   d. wann

SELF-TEST ANSWERS: KAPITEL 11

A. Answers will vary.

B. Answers will vary: Ich würde gern (jobben, durch Europa trampen, faulenzen, mich gern vom Streß erholen, nach Europa fliegen, eine Radtour machen, usw.).

C. 1. **immer** + comparative
2. a. immer mehr   b. immer größer

D. 1. Häuschen, Häuslein   3. Händchen
2. Büchlein   4. Schläfchen

E. Answers will vary: Ja, das wäre schön. / Wenn ich nur Geld (Zeit) hätte. / Das würde ich gern machen. / Das würde Spaß machen. / Dazu hätte ich keine Lust (Zeit).

F. 1. Hypothetical conclusions, wishes, polite requests
2. Trudi würde auch gern faulenzen.
3. Wenn die Sonne nur scheinen würde!
4. Würdest du noch eine Stunde bleiben?

G. 1. Add subjunctive endings to the simple-past stem. (an umlaut is added to the vowels **a, o,** or **u**).
2. a. er wäre   c. sie führen
   b. sie flöge   d. du bliebest

H. 1. The subjunctive is identical to the simple past forms.
2. a. sie lernte   b. du arbeitetest

I. 1. An umlaut is added to the simple past stem.
2. a. sie brächte   b. ich dächte
   c. wir hätten

J. 1. The subjunctive of modals is identical to the simple past, except that where there is an umlaut in the infinitive there is also an umlaut in the subjunctive (**wollen** and **sollen** do not have umlaut).
2. a. ich müßte   b. du könntest

K. 1. It consists of the subjunctive forms **hätte** or **wäre** + past participle.
2. a. wir wären gewesen
   b. er hätte gesungen
   c. ich hätte mitgemacht

L. 1. The past participle is identical with the infinitive.
2. Ich hätte das allein machen können.

M. 1. the condition (**wenn**-clause) and the conclusion
2. wenn   3. conditions of fact
4. conditions contrary to fact
5. a. *present time:* Christine würde nach Dänemark fliegen, wenn sie Zeit hätte. *or* Christine flöge nach Dänemark, wenn sie Zeit hätte.
   past time: Christine wäre nach Dänemark geflogen, wenn sie Zeit gehabt hätte.
   b. *present time:* Wenn ich Geld hätte, würde ich im Restaurant essen. *or* Wenn ich Geld hätte, äße ich im Restaurant.
   past time: Wenn ich Geld gehabt hätte, hätte ich im Restaurant gegessen.

N. 1. Ich täte das nicht.
2. Du würdest mir nicht glauben.
3. Wir könnten morgen fahren.
4. ...würde sie ein neues Auto kaufen.
5. ...wenn ich das gewußt hätte.
6. ...du könntest länger bleiben.

SELF-TEST ANSWERS: KAPITEL 12

A. Answers will vary: Ich glaube ja. / Ich nehme an. / Soviel ich weiß. / Hoffentlich. / Vielleicht. / Ich bin nicht sicher. / Warum fragst du?

B. 1. ein halb (*adj.*), die Hälfte (*noun*)
2. drei Viertel
3. ein Drittel

C. 1. **fraglich** = questionable
2. **täglich** = daily

D. 1. a form of **werden** plus an infinitive
2. final position

3. the auxiliary (**werden**), just after the infinitive
4. a. Inge wird uns helfen.
   b. Wirst du das wirklich machen?
   c. Michael sagt, daß er einen neuen Job suchen wird.

E. 1. infinitive form
2. last position, just after the dependent infinitive
3. a. Silke wird ihre Arbeit allein machen müssen.
   b. Wirst du bestimmt kommen können?

F. 1. When context makes clear that the events will take place in the future.
2. To express (1) present probability, (2) a supposition, and (3) a determination to do something.
3. a. Ich rufe dich heute abend an.
   b. Wir werden wohl um sieben essen.
   c. Ich werde meinen Freunden helfen.

G. 1. Let me do the dishes today.
2. Where did you leave your gloves again?
3. Unfortunately I have to have my cassette recorder repaired.
4. Let's go.

H. 1. last position
2. Ich werde es Sie morgen wissen lassen.

I. 1. gelassen; lassen   2. lassen
3. a. Warum hast du Kurt dein Auto fahren lassen?
   b. Ich habe meine Schlüssel zu Hause gelassen.

J. 1. It introduces a relative clause. It refers back to a noun or pronoun in the preceding clause.
2. in last position; the auxiliary follows the infinitive or the past participle

K. 1. Most forms are identical with the definite article forms.
2. a. denen   b. dessen   c. deren

L. 1. It depends on the gender and number of the noun to which it refers.
2. It depends on the relative pronoun's grammatical function in the clause (subject, direct object, etc.).
3. It depends on what case that preposition takes.

M. 1. der   4. dem   7. dem
   2. der   5. den   8. die
   3. deren   6. denen   9. das

SELF-TEST ANSWERS: KAPITEL 13

A. Answers will vary.
Enthusiastic: Ja gern. / O ja, das interessiert mich sehr. / Sicher. / Wenn du mich einlädst, gern. / Ja, ich freue mich darauf.
Unenthusiastic: In welches? / Ich habe keine Karte. / Vielleicht. Wer spielt? / Ich weiß nicht. / Ich habe eigentlich keine Zeit. / Ach, ich habe keine besondere Lust. / Nein, das interessiert mich nicht. / Wenn ich Zeit hätte, vielleicht.

B. 1. The subject performs the action expressed by the verb.
2. The subject is acted upon.

C. 1. a form of **werden** + past participle of the main verb
2. worden   3. worden
4. a. Das Essen wurde gerade gekocht.
   b. Das Badezimmer wurde jeden Tag geputzt.
   c. Das Bett wird gemacht werden.
   d. Der Brief wird heute noch geschrieben.
   e. Autos werden hier repariert.

D. 1. It is the object of the preposition **von.**
2. It is the object of the preposition **durch.**
3. a. durch   b. von

E. 1. the past participle plus **werden**
2. a. gemacht werden   b. repariert werden

F. 1. the same: dative
   a. I was not believed.
   b. He is being helped.

G. 1. It is dropped.
2. Es wurde bis spät in die Nacht getanzt.
3. Hier wird nur deutsch gesprochen.

H. 1. like a predicate adjective
2. apparent or statal passive
3. a. wird   b. ist   c. ist   d. wird

I. 1. (1) main verb (*to get, become, grow*)
   (2) auxiliary verb in the future tense (**werden** + dependent infinitive)
   (3) auxiliary verb in the passive voice (**werden** + past participle)

2. a. A trip to the *DDR* was planned. (passive, simple past)
   b. It's finally getting warmer. (main verb)
   c. He'll write to us. (future)

J. 1. (a) **man**
   (b) **sein + zu** + infinitive
   (c) reflexive construction
   (d) **sich lassen** + infinitive
   2. a. Man darf das nicht vergessen.
   b. Wie ist das zu erklären?
   c. In Deutschland verkaufen sich natürliche Sachen leichter.
   d. Mit der Chefin läßt sich gut reden.
   e. Da ist nichts zu machen.
   f. Man muß die Platte bestellen.
   g. Eine Programmiersprache ist nicht so leicht zu lernen.
   h. Blumenläden finden sich überall.
   i. Das Auto läßt sich leicht reparieren.

SELF-TEST ANSWERS: KAPITEL 14

A. Answers will vary: Politik, Wirtschaft, Sport, Musik, Theater, Literatur, Comics, Filme.

B. 1. subjunctive
   2. a. hätte   c. helfen würdest
   b. gesprochen hätte   d. könnte

C. 1. Time used depends on the tense used in the direct quotation: present time is used for present tense, past time for any past tense, and future time for future tense.
   2. a. Christoph hat gesagt, er wäre unschuldig.
   b. Gabi hat gesagt, sie hätte eine neue Stelle gefunden.
   c. Holger hat gesagt, er würde nicht streiken.

D. 1. Beate hat gefragt, ob Jürgen und Dirk mitkämen.
   2. Dirk hat gefragt, wie lange sie geblieben wären.
   3. Erika hat gefragt, ob der Urlaub schön gewesen wäre.

E. 1. Use the subjunctive form of the modal **sollen** + infinitive.
   2. a. Ingrid hat mir gesagt, ich sollte sie um vier treffen.
   b. Richard hat Christel gesagt, sie sollte Cola mitbringen.
   c. Tanja hat uns gesagt, wir sollten mitkommen.

F. 1. none
   2. in formal writing such as newspapers and literature
   3. third person singular (**er/es/sie**)

G. 1. It is made up of the infinitive stem plus subjunctive endings.
   2. a. sie fahre, führe   d. er habe, hätte
   b. er spreche, spräche   e. sie könne, könnte
   c. sie werde, würde   f. er müsse, müßte

H. 1. ich sei, wäre   3. Inge sei, wäre
   2. du seiest, wärest   4. wir seien, wären

I. 1. Special subjunctive forms of the auxiliaries **haben** and **sein** plus the past participle of the verb.
   2. a. sie habe gefunden, sie hätte gefunden
   b. er sei gelaufen, er wäre gelaufen
   c. sie habe gearbeitet, sie hätte gearbeitet
   d. er sei gegangen, er wäre gegangen

J. 1. finde   3. gemacht habe
   2. könne   4. gefahren sei

Proficiency Cards

For suggestions on how to use the Proficiency Cards, please see the Introduction to the Workbook/Lab Manual.

1. Warm-up

Walk around the room getting to know your fellow classmates. Give your name and ask for their names.

- ✂ -

2. Spelling names

Go back to people you have met and try to remember their names. Spell their last names: **Man buchstabiert das S C H M I D T, ja?**

- ✂ -

3. Getting acquainted

Walk around the classroom.

1. Talk to people whose names you remember. Ask their telephone numbers and addresses.
2. Introduce yourself to people you don't know.

- ✂ -

4. Asking for personal information

Make a list with the names of five people in the class.

1. Ask their telephone numbers and addresses.
2. Ask their ages.

5. Warm-up

You are at a party with your fellow classmates. Greet people and ask how they are.

---

6. Getting acquainted

You meet a fellow student for the first time. Get to know her/him. Find out what sports and activities she/he likes to do.

---

7. Meeting and greeting people

You meet a classmate on campus. Work out the following dialogue with a partner.

1. Greet her/him.
2. Ask how she/he is.
3. Ask what she/he is doing this afternoon.
4. Tell what you are doing.
5. Ask if she/he likes to play tennis.
6. Arrange a time to play together tomorrow.

---

8. Kaffeestunde

1. Talk about the different people in your class. Make comments.
2. Ask your partner what activities she/he will engage in today and at what time.

9. Warm-up

Your partner names a month or a geographical location. You must make an appropriate comment about the weather.

---

10. Discussing the weather

With a partner role-play the following situations. Each of you takes a role. Then reverse the roles.

1. You are visiting a friend far away from where you live. You are on the phone with someone from home. Tell her/him what the weather is like.
2. You meet a friend walking on campus during a blizzard/heat wave. Talk about the weather.
3. You see an interesting-looking person you want to meet on the beach. Start a conversation.
4. You are talking to a travel agent. You can't decide where you want to spend your next vacation. Ask about the weather in various places.

---

11. Describing people and objects

You are talking with a German friend. She/he wants to know about your first weeks at school. Tell her/him about:

1. a friend/a classmate.
2. the weather.
3. your room and its contents (size, color).

---

12. Kaffeestunde

1. Talk about the activities you engage in regularly.
2. Talk about the weather.
3. With your partner, look around the room. Comment on a few of the objects you see.
4. Comment on people's moods yesterday.

13. Warm-up

Pretend you are on a busy street. You are looking for a store. Walk around the room. When your instructor signals, stop. A person close to you will ask you what you are looking for. Tell her/him. Walk around until your instructor signals again. Use the name of a different store each time.

14. Determining needs

You invite a classmate back to your room or apartment for dinner.

1. She/he makes comments on your room/apartment.
2. Ask her/him what she/he likes to eat.
3. Either you don't have what she/he has mentioned or what you have is not fresh.
4. She/he asks if there is a grocery store nearby.
5. Make a list of what you will buy together for dinner.

15. Describing objects

You and your friend are in a large department store. You need to buy three items for your room. You look at different items and express your opinion about them. Your friend disagrees with you about everything.

16. Kaffeestunde

1. Ask your partner about what she/he likes to eat and what she/he normally buys every week at the grocery store.
2. Ask your partner about what she/he needs to buy.

17. Warm-up

Sit in a circle of five. Each person:

1. names a subject she/he is studying.
2. says whether or not it is her/his major or minor.
3. tells what work she/he must prepare now—either a test or a report.

---

18. Getting acquainted

You meet a fellow student in the library.

1. Ask what she/he is doing here.
2. Ask which classes she/he is taking.
3. Ask what her/his major is.
4. Ask if she/he would like to go out for coffee.
5. She/he has a test tomorrow and must study.

---

19. Talking with fellow students

With a partner role-play the following situations. When you are finished, switch roles.

1. You are interested in a class that your friend is taking. Ask about what work is required for the class. Ask if you can borrow her/his notes.
2. You are trying to find someone who will lend you her/his notes for last week's German class. Everyone you meet has a different reason for not lending them to you.
3. You and your friend/roommate are discussing what you can, should, want to and are supposed to do tonight. You decide however to go drink some coffee and listen to music.

---

20. Kaffeestunde

1. Ask your partner about her/his studies.
2. Ask your partner about her/his family.
3. Use the following phrases to start conversations with your partner:

> **Ich kann ...**
> **Ich soll ...**
> **Magst du ... ?**
> **Ich muß heute ...**
> **Darfst du ... ?**
> **Möchtest du ... ?**

21. Warm-up

Sit in a circle of four. Two people stand in the center. One of the two asks questions and the other answers. The person who runs out of things to say first (either questions or answers) sits down and is replaced by another person. In the new round, question and answer roles are reversed.

---

22. Discussing vacation plans

You are going home during the next vacation for someone's birthday. A friend/your roommate is interested in going with you.

1. She/he wants to know how you are getting home and where she/he can stay.
2. Tell her/him about the weather.
3. Tell her/him how she/he can get around town.
4. She/he asks what there is to do in your town.
5. She/he asks what you are giving the person whose birthday it is. She/he wants to give a gift as well.

She/he may ask you for further information.

---

23. Convincing a friend to participate in activities

You are trying to convince a friend of yours to go with you as an exchange student to Austria. Tell her/him what you know about Austria and what she/he can do there.

---

24. Kaffeestunde

1. Ask about your partner's daily routine.
2. Ask where your partner is going on her/his next vacation and with whom.
3. Discuss public transportation here. (Compare to Europe)

25. Warm-up

You are a server at a party. Walk around the room. When your instructor signals, stop and offer the person closest to you something to eat or drink. She/he will politely accept or decline.

---

26. Ordering in a restaurant

Role-play the following situations in groups of three. Each person takes a role. When you are finished, switch roles.

1. You are at a restaurant with a friend of yours. You are a vegetarian and she/he can't eat salt or sugar. Order accordingly.
2. You and your partner are in your favorite restaurant. Order what you like to eat most. Unfortunately the waiter doesn't have what you want.

---

27. Reporting about recent events

Your friend/roommate has just returned from a wonderful evening out with a special person. Ask her/him about it.

---

28. Kaffeestunde

1. Ask your partner about the last meal she/he had in a restaurant.
2. Talk about natural foods, health food stores, and restaurants that you know about.
3. Ask your partner what she/he likes and doesn't like about the town or city your college/university is in.
4. Talk and ask about the last meal you had in a natural foods restaurant.
5. Talk about the clothes your classmates are wearing today.

1. Walk around the room. When your instructor signals, stop. Tell the person closest to you what you are doing this afternoon and invite her/him to join you.
2. With a partner, list five things you consider characteristic of life in German-speaking countries and five you consider characteristic of life where you live. Share your ideas with another group.

✂

30. Describing spatial location

a. Draw your room

b. Draw your partner's room

When you have finished drawing your own room, describe it to your partner without showing her/him your drawing. She/he must draw according to how you describe the location of various objects. When she/he is finished, compare drawings.

Fold Here

Fold Here

31. Discussing vacation activities

You meet a young German traveler in a café. With a partner, prepare your conversation.

1. Ask her/him where she/he is from.
2. She/he is from Munich.
3. You were in Europe last year. Your family goes there once a year.
4. She/he asks why you go so often.
5. Your sister lives near Munich.
6. She/he asks you what you do when you are at your sister's.
7. You go into Munich everyday. On Sundays you go to the mountains. Your family likes to go hiking in the Alps.
8. Ask her/him where she/he is going to in the States.
9. She/he was in New York a week ago. On Monday she/he is going to the Rockies. She/he likes to hike and will be hiking four weeks in the mountains.
10. You think that's great.
11. She/he invites you to come along.
12. Unfortunately, you have to study for tests.
13. Ask her/his name, address, and phone number for the next time you are in Europe.

---

32. Kaffeestunde

1. Think of how you would complete each of the following phrases. Use one of the completed sentences to start a conversation with your partner.

> **Ich denke oft an ...**
> **Ich rede gern über ...**
> **Ich habe Angst vor ...**
> **Meine Großmutter erzählt immer von ...**
> **Ich höre mit ... auf. / Ich höre auf mit ...**
> **Ich helfe meinen Freunden gern bei ...**

2. Ask your partner what she/he will be doing:
   a. next Monday.
   b. Saturday evening.
   c. in a year.

3. Ask what she/he was doing a year ago.

Fold Here

Fold Here

33. Warm-up

Sit in a group of five. One person names a room. Each of the others must name an activity or household chore that is done in that room.

---

34. Discussing housing (1)

You see an ad in the newspaper for a room to rent. You go to see the room and ask the landlord questions about the house. Ask:

1. how many floors and rooms the house has.
2. if there is a garden, a balcony, a basement.
3. where the kitchen is.
4. where your room is and where the bathroom is.
5. which other rooms you can use.
6. how much the rent is.

---

35. Discussing housing (2)

You are a real-estate agent with a beautiful house to sell. Describe it for your partner who is a reluctant customer. Your glowing description finally convinces her/him to buy.

---

36. Kaffeestunde

1. With a partner, make comments about objects in the classroom and what people are wearing.
2. Think of how you would complete the following phrases. Use one of your completed sentences to start a conversation with your partner.

 Eines Tages ...
 Trotz ...
 Während ...
 Wegen ...
 Statt ...

3. Point out various objects in the room to a partner. **Wessen ... ist das? Wem gehört das?** She/he will answer.

37. Warm-up

Six people participate in a quiz game on Switzerland. Form teams of three and prepare seven questions on Switzerland. The teams take turns asking their questions.

---

38. Discussing one's health

With a partner, role-play the following conversations.

1. Your partner doesn't feel well. She/he has been up all night cramming for an exam. Ask her/him what's wrong.
2. You went skiing last weekend. It was very sunny and you fell quite a bit. Your partner asks you on Monday how you are feeling.
3. Your roommate has all the symptoms of pneumonia. Ask her/him how she/he feels and suggest she/he see a doctor.
4. You are a doctor. A patient comes to you not feeling well. She/he complains of many different symptoms. You suspect stress and suggest changes in her/his daily routine.

---

39. Comparing academic and personal achievement

You and your partner are members of a university admissions committee. You have to decide which of the following three students you will award an athletic scholarship to.

	Noten	Tennis	Anderes
Brita Feyler	3,7	* *	Preis für Computer-Programm
Günther Weyl	3,5	* * *	spielt Schach / Hilft Kindern beim Lesen
Peter Weiß	3,2	* * * *	Präsident der Klasse

---

40. Kaffeestunde

1. Talk about your daily routine.
2. **Was muß man machen um _____ zu werden?**
3. Talk about activities you like to do the most.
4. Think about a friend you know well. Your partner will ask you questions comparing the two of you, e.g., **Ist er/sie älter?**

41. Warm-up

Sit in a circle of five. One person starts a story by completing the sentence: **Als Frau Schmidt mit dem Bus zur Arbeit fahren wollte, ...** The other students must each contribute a sentence to the story's continuation.

---

42. Interviewing for a job

You are interviewing a prospective candidate for a sales position in your computer store. Your partner is the prospective applicant. She/he has had summer sales experience during college and has a degree in computer programming. You think he is the right person for the job but she/he is reluctant to work Saturdays. Ask her/him about:

1. her/his educational background.
2. her/his previous work experience.
3. why she/he wants to go into sales.
4. working on Saturdays.

Offer her/him some interesting incentives to ensure that she/he accepts the position.

---

43. Talking about past events

You are a television talk show host. Your guest is a well-known film star. Ask her/him about her/his life. Be sure to ask specifically about:

1. her/his life before she became a film star.
2. her/his career before she/he became famous.
3. the highlights of her/his career.
4. any interesting stories she/he would like to share.

---

44. Kaffeestunde

1. Tell your partner about a funny incident that happened when you were young.
2. Think of how you would complete each of the following sentences. Then use one of the sentences to start a conversation with your partner.

> **Als ich jung war,** dachte ich ...
> hatte ich ...
> wollte ich ...
> mußte ich ...

45. Warm-up

Sit in a circle of five. Each of you says what you would rather be doing if you weren't studying. The others may ask you about your plans.

✂

46. Talking about hypothetical situations

You and your friend/roommate are talking about how you would live differently if you were rich and famous. Discuss the advantages and disadvantages.

✂

47. Expressing polite requests or wishes

Role-play the following situations with your partner. When you are finished reverse roles.

1. Go and talk to your instructor. You have a difficult paper to write and you don't know how to approach it.
2. You are sick. Ask your friend/roommate for a glass of water. You also want something to eat.
3. You need to borrow five dollars from your aunt/uncle. Your aunt/uncle is hard of hearing and doesn't always hear what you say.
4. You want to ask a new group of friends if you can go to the movies with them.
5. Your grandmother/grandfather has to go to the bank. Suggest that she/he should be going. She/he is also hard of hearing and doesn't always take kindly to suggestions.
6. You have been paying your own tuition but you couldn't work last summer and you need money. Ask a relative if you could borrow money from her/him for next semester's tuition.

✂

48. Kaffeestunde

Think of how you would complete the following phrases. Then use one of the sentences to start a conversation with your partner.

1. **Könnten Sie ... ?**
   Dürfte ich ... ?
   Ich wollte ...
   Sie sollten ...
   Müßte ich ... ?
2. **Wenn jetzt Ferien wären, ...**
   Wenn jetzt Samstag abend wäre, ...

49. Warm-up

Try to sell something you no longer need. Your partner is reluctant to buy it so you must convince her/him of the good qualities it has and of the advantages of owning it.

✂

50. Discussing future intentions (1)

You want to talk to the president of a company but must arrange for an appointment with an assistant. Convince the assistant why you need to talk with the president.

✂

51. Discussing future intentions (2)

For groups of five.

You are employees of a very successful company. Decide:

1. what your company makes.
2. who's who in the company.
3. a name for your company.

Once you have decided these issues, get up and choose a partner from another group. Talk about your company to her/him.

When you have finished, re-join your company and discuss your goals for the next five years.

✂

52. Kaffeestunde

1. Make comments about different people and objects in the classroom. **Das ist die Frau, die ...**
2. Talk about a company you know well.
3. Ask your partner to tell you about:
   - a. a film she/he would like to see.
   - b. a book she/he would like to read.
   - c. a trip she/he would like to take.

53. Warm-up

Sit in a circle of five. Each person tells about a film or television program she/he has seen recently.

✂

54. Discussing cultural events

You finally meet someone who loves cultural events as much as you do.

1. Ask her/his preferences.
2. Ask about the last event she/he attended.
3. Invite her/him to [the opera] next week.
4. She/he is reluctant and asks you what is playing.
5. You tell her/him that it is [Mozart's *Magic Flute*].
6. It's her/his favorite opera. She/he'd love to go.
7. Arrange a time and place to meet beforehand.

✂

55. Getting acquainted

You travel to the German Democratic Republic for the first time. Your partner is a young student you meet in a café.

1. Introduce yourself.
2. Ask about where and what she/he studies.
3. Ask about her/his family.
4. Ask about life in the German Democratic Republic.
6. She/he wants to know what you think of the country.
7. She/he invites you to meet her/his friends.

✂

56. Kaffeestunde

1. Talk about a celebration or activity you or your friends are arranging. Tell who will do the different tasks.
2. Talk about what you have learned about the German Democratic Republic.

57. Warm-up

Tell a partner why you read a certain newspaper or magazine. Your partner has one she/he likes better and tells you why.

58. Reporting what another person says

With a partner, role-play the following dialogue. You are listening to a friend complain about her/his roommate. The roommate always says things she/he doesn't do. Listen to the friend talk and ask questions where appropriate. The roommate says she/he:

1. will clean the room but never does.
2. will buy food but never does.
3. will turn the stereo down but never does.
4. will take you out to dinner but never does.
5. will pick up her/his dirty clothes but never does.
6. [...]

When you have had enough of your friend's complaints, suggest that she/he find a new roommate.

59. Assessing cultural acclimatization

You are a journalist for a major West German newsweekly. You are interviewing a guest worker about her/his impressions of life in the Federal Republic of Germany. Be sure to ask her/him:

1. about working conditions.
2. about cultural differences.
3. about family life.

60. Kaffeestunde

1. Ask your partner if she/he would like to study in a German-speaking country for a year. Why?
2. Talk about what you have learned about the German-speaking countries this year.
3. Talk about ways in which you can continue to learn more about the German language and culture.